Collected Poems of Lenore Kandel

Collected Poems of Lenore Kandel

with a preface by
Diane di Prima

North Atlantic Books
Berkeley, California

Published by North Atlantic Books
P.O. Box 12327
Berkeley, California 94712

Jacket cover, jacket flap, and frontispiece photographs courtesy of the Estate of Lenore Kandel. All efforts to determine the names of the photographers were unsuccessful. If you have any information about the photographers, please contact North Atlantic Books.

Cover and interior design by Larry Van Dyke

Printed in the United States of America

Collected Poems of Lenore Kandel is sponsored by the Society for the Study of Native Arts and Sciences, a nonprofit educational corporation whose goals are to develop an educational and cross-cultural perspective linking various scientific, social, and artistic fields; to nurture a holistic view of arts, sciences, humanities, and healing; and to publish and distribute literature on the relationship of mind, body, and nature.

North Atlantic Books' publications are available through most bookstores. For further information, visit our website at www.northatlanticbooks.com or call 800-733-3000.

Library of Congress Cataloging-in-Publication Data

Kandel, Lenore.
[Poems]
Collected poems of Lenore Kandel / Lenore Kandel ; with a preface by Diane di Prima.
p. cm.
Summary: "Collected Poems of Lenore Kandel is an evocative and startlingly original collection of poems (including one prose short story) by one of the most controversial poets of the Sixties"--Provided by publisher.
ISBN 978-1-58394-372-4
I. Title.
PS3561.A46 2012
811'.54--dc23

2011029481

1 2 3 4 5 6 7 8 SHERIDAN 17 16 15 14 13 12

Acknowledgments

Thanks to Vicki Pollack for the many hours she spent gathering the poems in this book, to Evan Karp for transcribing them and putting them in order, and to Lisa Kot for working with the publisher to make this book happen.

Contents

Preface by Diane di Prima xiii
Introduction xvii

I. The Love Book (1966)

God/Love Poem 3
To Fuck with Love Phase I 5
To Fuck with Love Phase II 6
To Fuck with Love Phase III 7

II. Word Alchemy (1967)

Circus 11
Poster 11
Beast Parade 12
Love in the Middle of the Air 14
Invocation and Clowns, Dance of the Bareback Riders 15
Freak Show and Finale 16
Invocation for Maitreya 17
Enlightenment Poem 18
Now Vision 19
Farewell to Fancy 21
Were–Poem 22
Rose/Vision 23
Age of Consent 24
Lady/Poem 25

Stonedream 26
Emerald Poem 27
First They Slaughtered the Angels 28
Joy Song 32
Eros/Poem 33
Hard Core Love 34
Love-Lust Poem 35
Peyote Walk 37
Vision of the Skull of the Prophet 39
Poem for Tyrants 40
The Farmer, the Sailor 41
Bus Ride 42
Anatomy Note 43
Love Song for Snow White 44
Bedsong for Her 45
Poem for Peter 46
Three/Love Poem 47
Melody for Married Men 48
Spring 61 49
Small Prayer for Falling Angels 51
Naked I Have Known You 52
Kirby/Poem 54
Junk/Angel 55
Blues for Sister Sally 56
Morning Song 58
Telephone from a Madhouse 60
In Transit 64
In the Comics 67
Horoscope 70
Poem for Perverts 72

III. Poems from Three Penny Press Chapbooks (1959)

"All I have in the world" 77
Apogee 79
"Clearly beloved, we are huddled here together" 80
"Hey, hey, I have a universe to share with you" 81
"Home is where you find it" 82
"The hot wind blows and I wish I could blow with it" 83
"Hungry as a sulky child nothing suits me" 84
"I gave you all the rains" 85
"I have chosen for my guide the gray wind" 86
"I have fallen in love with the wind" 87
"I thought you were a man" 88
"The love I had for you, baby" 89
"Loving and love being the reason behind it all" 90
"Mountains and cities and pitfalls and" 91
"My beloved has a hundred faces . . ." 92
"My love gave me an orange tree" 93
"Oh, my beloved . . ." 94
"Our morning is afternoon" 95
A Passing Dragon 97
"Pigeons always spell New York to me" 98
"Slipping into my heart as once" 99
"Such a tomcat then" 102
"There is a hole in my heart" 103
"This is my world" 104
The Twenty Nine Hungers of God 106
"You are like a lion" 107
"You there! You with the loneliness" 108
"Your conversation, friend" 109

IV. Poems from Little Magazines and Broadsides (1960–2004)

Speaking of . . . 113
"Baby listen, I am the missionary of love" 115
Wonder Wander 116
Poem for Ann 117
"Rocking in the rain" 118
"Steazoned in heazell, by candlelight" 119
Rebirth 120
Changeling 121
Scarey Song 122
Watching the Veiled Moon 123
Witch Song 124
Grey-Beast 125
Woods Poem 126
Someday When We Are Strangers 127
"I have never seen a nightingale" 128
City Night 129
"Ah love, I had not meant to leave" 130
In the Bitter Hours of Night 131
Hero the Rider 132
The Time of the Golden Bull 133
Afternoon of a Phoenix 138
Phoenix Song 139
girl story 140
Fog-Bound 141
Old Lady Poem 142
No Clock No Time 143
Poem for a Long-Gone Lover 146
Grant Avenue 147
"I reveal my belly to delight" 148
"afraid to sleep alone" 149
Small Hours Poem 150

Storm July 151
"sweet love I have lost my words lost my praises" 152
Epilogue 153
"my love the fisherman comes back smelling of salt dying" 154
Museum Concert 155
Fuck/Angel 156
Poem for Sunday Riders 157
"If all day long you had a perfectly beautiful Tuesday" 158
Rose Dream 159
Vernal Equinox Forecast—1968 160
"old men" 161
Hawaiian Mountain 165
Hymn to Maitreya in America 167
Muir Beach Mythology/September 170
Excerpt from a Prayer Wheel 171
Dead Billy 173
dry man 174
prayer on the wind 175
seven of velvet 176
Quantum Choreography 177
Everyday Magic 178
the pot bird story 179
Gregory 180
A Place to Stand 181

V. Unpublished Works

Afterword 185
American Dreams 186
Angel 190
Cherokee 191
CircumLocation 192
Dancers Poem 193
A Definition of Love 194

Dope Poem 195
Excerpt 196
"He's the red-handed saint of temptations" 197
Holding 198
"I would not shackle love" 199
If I Am Holy— 200
"I'm writing poems on you" 201
Incarnation of Light 202
Island 203
"it was your mind that caught me" 204
Levels 205
"love is an art for angels" 206
Map of the Moon 207
The Mathematics of Love 208
Memorabilia 209
night passage 210
Nostalgia 211
Open Channel 212
"the phoenix sings once in five hundred years" 213
Remembrance of Saint John the Dwarf 214
Seven of Stars 215
Songs of the Blue-Light Dakini 216
"sweet love, there are no comparisons" 217
Thunder Calliope 218
Where It's At: A Melody For Breath 219
Winter Solstice 1975 220

VI. A Fictional Sketch (1953)
The Boy with the Innocent Eyes 223

Notes 229
Alphabetical List of Works 235
About the Author 241

Preface

INVITATION TO THE JOURNEY: An Homage for Lenore Kandel

When I came from the East Coast to San Francisco on a reading tour in the spring of 1968, the woman I stayed with ruled a magic kingdom, pristine as the heart of a jewel. She would have said emerald. I, perhaps, sapphire. Or ruby, for I dwelt in fire. She in the Heart of Venus/Isis; she dwelt in earth and in the middle of the air. I sought shelter from her, and she gave me shelter. I looked to leave the burning sidewalks of my broken stone island, she gave me welcome. Gave me a glass key to one of the gates of this four-walled city/temple.

For several months, I had lost my power to dream. This is fact. Perhaps I set out on this Quest because I was no longer dreaming. I woke in the morning with no treasures from the kingdoms of Night. Then one afternoon I returned to her apartment from the beveled glass and flashing ocean light of the San Francisco streets, to find the room Lenore had lent me had been changed: clouds hung in the air, and sharp bits of mica flashed and swam before me as if space were some viscous substance. Something not empty. Amongst the swirls of smoke Lenore manifested smiling—she simply showed up in that place, brass candle-holder in the shape of a gryphon in one hand, a stick of some herb or incense in the other. "I think you'll dream tonight" she said, and I did. And did again and again—for more than ten years after that my dreams fed me, guided me.

Fragile beauty we held in our hands. The Time, the Place, the Assembly. Brittle as spun glass, the slightest wind could send these hills and towers tumbling, and did. But not then. Not yet.

One night this lady from a barely remembered Age dressed as queens once dressed set out, long black leather coat pulled over some bright gown; she drew a dark casque over the jewels that held her hair, mounted a motorcycle behind her dark lover and they disappeared. Flying into the night to join their kin, to join the Dance, Dr. John officiating. I watched them from her window.

Another night, at a free dinner and dance thrown by the Diggers for a couple of thousand friends and newcomers, I was helping cook and serve an entire sheep, till I was drawn away from my work by a new hallucinogen someone had put in my hand. When it became clear the drug would have its way, I left the dance, took a cab home. Lenore came back hours later to find me wrangling a potted tree down her winding staircase. This tree, I explained, had been talking to me. It was feeling claustrophobic. Its top leaves were touching her ceiling, and it wanted, it *needed* to go higher. The choices were: to cut a hole in the ceiling or to move the plant. I had wisely opted for the latter. Lenore eased her tree out of my arms and got both me and the greenery back inside.

We exchanged drugs and the knowledge of drugs as we traded far memory and our knowledge of ritual and healing. Thinking none of it strange. I brought vision-substance from Millbrook, she offered hashish that smelled like the earth of some ancestral land and crumbled in my hand. Without hesitance or guilt: the Road we knew led only from Vision to further Vision.

Lenore was many things to the men and women of this realm. Young as she was then, she was clearly the one to whom many turned. For advice, for healing. Some days I would sit beside her and watch and learn. The women of her tribe came by to bead and to mourn, to cook or sew while they talked of lost loves, of children and abortions. The men dropped in with barely hatched dreams for a new society, with manuscripts and music, weapons and possibilities.

One poet brought the rich dark wines of the California hills, and the latest issue of his literary journal. He was stopping to say goodbye, was moving north. His lady would stay behind in San Francisco. His choice or hers? I wondered. No one said. Then he was gone, and someone else was at the door; someone to whom I wasn't introduced handed Lenore a stack of neatly bundled cash for the "Free Bank". This was a shoe-box on her refrigerator, full of money. Anyone could come and take what they needed and anyone could add what they were moved to add.

Bill, Lenore's lover—who was later "Sweet William" and a Hell's Angel—talked long one night about his vision of "Free City" the heavenly city burning in his mind. He was passionate, if (I thought) a little vague. But he *knew* it had to happen, it could and must happen, and *at once.* Lenore and I exchanged glances, knowing as we did, that perhaps it would take a while, perhaps it wouldn't, couldn't, be quite as quick as all that.

After a week or so, when I left this City of tribal dreams, Bill drove me to the airport in his truck. As we left the houses behind, he told me to look out the window: a cavalcade of motorcycles flanked the pickup: ahead, beside and behind us. The Angels were escorting the poet to her flight.

In two months I returned to stay—but that is another story. The part that is relevant here is that it was Lenore in that same pickup who came to the airport to meet me—and the passel of kids and "grown-ups" I'd brought along—to drive us to our new home, a fourteen-room house I'd rented in the Haight.

All the power of that time is in these poems. The piercing innocence that led up to it. The power and joy of the flesh, of fellowship, and drugs. Magic doors leading to countries we barely had time to map. The Invitation to Journey—that is here, too. What that Quest was we still don't know, can't say. Though we know something of the price that was paid, and that too is recorded here. Lenore doesn't flinch or look away from the pain, the destruction that was foisted on her. On her comrades and mine. Her world and mine.

It is here for you, reader, cartographer. Further Traveler. The Invitation is open; the Voyage continues.

—Diane di Prima

Introduction

Poetry is never compromise. It is the manifestation/translation of a vision, an illumination, an experience. If you compromise your vision you become a blind prophet.

There is no point today in that poetry which exists mainly as an exercise in dexterity. Craft is valuable insofar as it serves as a brilliant midwife for clarity, beauty, vision; when it becomes enamored of itself it produces word masturbation.

The poems I write are concerned with all aspects of the creature and of that total universe through which he moves. The aim is toward the increase of awareness. It may be awareness of the way a bird shatters the sky with his flight or awareness of the difficulty and necessity of trust or awareness of the desire for awareness and also the fear of awareness. This may work through beauty or shock or laughter but the direction is always toward clear sight, both interior and exterior.

This demands honesty within the poet and the poem. An honesty sometimes joyful and sometimes painful, whether to the poet or the reader or both. Two poems of mine, published as a small book, deal with physical love and the invocation, recognition, and acceptance of the divinity in man through the medium of physical love. In other words, it feels good. It feels so good that you can step outside your private ego and share the grace of the universe. This simple and rather self-evident statement, enlarged and exampled poetically, raised a furor difficult to believe. A large part of the furor was caused by the poetic usage of certain four-letter words of Anglo-Saxon origin instead of the substitution of gentle euphemisms.

This brings up the question of poetic language. Whatever is language is poetic language and if the word required by the poet does not exist in his known language then it is up to him to discover it. The only proviso can be that the word be the correct word as demanded by the poem and only the poet can be the ultimate judge of that.

Euphemisms chosen by fear are a covenant with hypocrisy and will immediately destroy the poem and eventually destroy the poet.

Any form of censorship, whether mental, moral, emotional, or physical, whether from the inside out or the outside in, is a barrier against self-awareness.

Poetry is alive because it is a medium of vision and experience.

It is not necessarily comfortable.

It is not necessarily safe.

Poetry has moved out of the classroom and into the street and thus brought about a flow of cross-pollination, many of the fruits of which are viable in both mediums. Academia tended to breed the fear of offense, i.e., that which might offend someone. Visions and language both were often dwarfed and muted, the poem too often becoming a vehicle for literary gymnastics.

Street poetry avoids the fear-trap, but too often loses its vision through a lack of clarity, through sloppiness, through a lack of the art of the craft.

Poetry as poetry has no need to be classified in either of the above pigeonholes nor in any other. It exists. It cannot exist in the company of censorship.

When a poet censors his vision he no longer tells the truth as he sees it. When he censors the language of the poem he does not use those words which, to him, are the most perfect words to be used. This self-stunting results in an artificial limitation imposed on an art whose direction is beyond the limits of the conceivable.

There are no barriers to poetry or prophecy; by their nature they are barrier-breakers, bursts of perceptions, lines into infinity. If a poet lies about his vision he lies about himself and in himself; this produces a true barrier. When a poet through fearful expediency uses language other than that which is perfect to the poem he becomes a person of fearful expediency.

When an outside agency takes it upon itself to attempt the censorship of poetry it is censoring the acceptance of truth and the leap toward revelation.

When a society becomes afraid of its poets, it is afraid of itself. A society afraid of itself stands as another definition of hell. A poem that is written and published becomes available to those who choose to read it. This seems to me to imply one primary responsibility on the part of the poet—that he tell the truth as he sees it. That he tell it as beautifully, as amazingly, as he can; that he ignite his own sense of wonder; that he work alchemy within the language—these are the form and existence of poetry itself.

A good part of the audience for modern poetry is young. We move in a world where the polarities and possibilities of life and death exist as constant consciousness. Once the concept and availability of overkill was made public knowledge the aura of the possibility of cosmic death became visible. There have been eras when the young could slip softly into their elders lives, when if they wanted to ignore the deeper issues of humanity, of man's relationship to man, it was made easy for them. This is not such a time and the choices of the young are deep and hard. At eighteen the young men must decide whether they will enter into the national pastime of death. A great many of the young are choosing to manifest a different way of life, one motivated toward pleasure, toward enlightenment, and toward mutual concern, instead of accepting the world of war and personal despair which has been offered them by the majority of their elders.

There are heavy choices to make and there is no avoidance possible.

Those who read modern poetry do so for pleasure, for insight, sometimes for counsel. The least they can expect is that the poet who shares his visions and experiences with them do so with no hypocrisy. To compromise poetry through expediency is the soft, small murder to the soul.

—Lenore Kandel, San Francisco 1967

I.

The Love Book

(1966)

God/Love Poem

there are no ways of love but/beautiful/
I love you all of them

I love you / your cock in my hand
stirs like a bird
in my fingers
as you swell and grow hard in my hand
forcing my fingers open
with your rigid strength
you are beautiful / you are beautiful
you are a hundred times beautiful
I stroke you with my loving hands
pink-nailed long fingers
I caress you
I adore you
my finger-tips . . . my palms . . .
your cock rises and throbs in my hands
a revelation / as Aphrodite knew it

there was a time when gods were purer
/I can recall nights among the honeysuckle
our juices sweeter than honey
/ we were the temple and the god entire/

I am naked against you
and I put my mouth on you slowly
I have longing to kiss you
and my tongue makes worship on you
you are beautiful

your body moves to me
flesh to flesh
skin sliding over golden skin
as mine to yours
   my mouth   my tongue   my hands
my belly and my legs
against your mouth   your love
sliding . . . sliding . . .
our bodies move and join
unbearably

your face above me
   is the face of all the gods
      and beautiful demons
your eyes . . .

      love touches love
      the temple and the god
      are one

To Fuck with Love   Phase I

to fuck with love   to change the temperature of the air
passing two strangers into one osmotic angel
beyond the skin
(grows in my hands
like a tree)

miracle miracle
out of the burning bush
I understand the lingam ladies bruising their softest flesh
in unassuageable worship
(like a tree)
positions and pleasures of need my body
transforms into one enormous mouth
between my legs
suckfucking oh that lovely cock
big grand and terrible
the upthrust implement of love
I taste the mouthpores of my body
cocksucker in heavenly
the tongue between my thighs spreading my legs to scream
and burst I burst I burst
he moves from me to me and then
plunging (big grand most terrible) into and all of me
can help but shriek
YES YES YES this is what I wanted this
beautiful
he explodes volcano tipped inside me my veins drip sperm
my GOD the worship that it is to fuck!

To Fuck with Love   Phase II

to fuck with love—
to know the tremor of your flesh within my own—
          feeling of thick sweet juices running wild
          sweat bodies tight and tongue to tongue

I am all those ladies of antiquity enamored of the sun
my cunt is honeycomb we are covered with come and honey
we are covered with each other my skin is the taste of you

          fuck—the fuck of love-fuck—the yes entire—
          love out of ours—the cock in the cunt fuck—
          the fuck of pore into pore—the smell of fuck
          taste it—love dripping from skin to skin—
          tongue at the doorways—cock god in heaven—
          love blooms entire universe—I/you
reflected in the golden mirror we are avatars of
                                                  Krishna and Radha
          pure love-lust of godhead   beauty unbearable
                carnal incarnate

I am the god-animal, the mindless cuntdeity   the hegod-animal
is over me, through me   we are become one total angel
united in fire   united in semen and sweat   united in lovescream

          sacred our acts and our actions
          sacred our parts and our persons

sacred the sacred cunt!
sacred the sacred cock!
miracle!   miracle!   sacred the primal miracle!

          sacred the god-animal, twisting and wailing

                sacred the beautiful fuck

To Fuck with Love   Phase III

to fuck with love
to love with all the heat and wild of fuck
the fever of your mouth devouring all my secrets and my alibis
leaving me pure   burned into oblivion
the sweetness UNENDURABLE
        mouth   barely touching   mouth

                nipple to nipple we touched
                and were transfixed
                by a flow of energy
                beyond anything I have ever known

                we TOUCHED!

                and two days later
                my hand embracing your semen-dripping cock
                AGAIN!

                the energy
                indescribable
                almost   unendurable

the barrier of noumenon-phenomenon
        transcended
the circle   momentarily complete
                                        the balance of forces
                                            perfect

                lying together, our bodies slipping into love
                that never have slipped out
                I kiss your shoulder and it reeks of lust
                the lust of erotic angels fucking the stars

and shouting their insatiable joy over heaven
the lust of comets colliding in celestial hysteria
the lust of hermaphroditic deities doing
inconceivable things to each other and
SCREAMING DELIGHT over the entire universe
and beyond
and we lie together, our bodies wet and burning, and
we WEEP we WEEP we WEEP the incredible tears
that saints and holy men shed in the presence
of their own incandescent gods

I have whispered love into every orifice of your body
as you have done
to me

my whole body is turning into a cuntmouth
my toes my hands my belly my breasts my shoulders my eyes
you fuck me continually with your tongue you look
with your words with your presence
we are transmuting
we are as soft and warm and trembling
as a new gold butterfly

the energy
indescribable
almost unendurable

at night sometimes I see our bodies glow

II.

Word Alchemy

(1967)

Circus

Poster

VENGEFUL EXHIBIT OF ANGELS!
INDECENT EXPOSURE! TRUMPETS!
DANCE OF THE JELLYBEAN GIRLS!

INESCAPABLE PEARL BLOSSOMS
TORTURE!
SWEETHEARTS!

love lyrics of the homesick tiger
the secret mating dance of
everybody

ALL dreams ARE true
THIS is a dream
THIS is TRUE

Beast Parade

love me, love my elephant . . .
        never mock a tiger
        never tease a lion
        you and your mother
        are kinfolk to the jungle

SEE THE SPANGLED LEOPARD LADY!
watch the elephant ballet, eight thousand pounds of meat cavorting
for your languished eye
cumbersome feet used for nefarious purposes
(consider umbrellas in *your* grandma's hollowed foot)
        !WATCH!
        the gorilla takes a leak
        the monkey masturbates
                how life-like . . .
        SEE the
                TIGer
                    SWITCH his
                        TAIL!
the leopard lady walks her sister on a shining leash
        the eye
        of the tiger
        hides
        behind the sign of scorpio

HERE BE STRANGE BEASTES AND UNKNOWN LANDES
        HERE BE LIONS
        exhausted
        from the smell of popcorn

high in the altitude of the furthest Everest of benches and
everywhere and down to the very front row seats
the eye of the beast shines from contorted craniums
struggling between homo the human sapiens circa Now and
that dark beast before

turtle-man sparrow lady
tiger in a dress-suit monkey in a sweater
beetle-man, ape-man, poodle-man, snake-man, horse-man,
bull-man, camel-man, goat-man, man-man

  !STOP!
  observe your brethren, guard your true love
  these are dark latitudes
  and the ringmaster has wings
  let the parade begin!
  love me, love my elephant . . .
    love my tiger . . .
    love my anything . . .
    get in line . . .

Love in the Middle of the Air

CATCH ME!
    I love you, I trust you,
    I love you
CATCH ME!
    catch my left foot, my right
    foot, my hand!
    here I am hanging by my teeth
    300 feet up in the air and
CATCH ME!
    here I come, flying without wings,
    no parachute, doing a double triple
    super flip-flop somersault
    RIGHT UP HERE WITHOUT A
    SAFETY NET AND
CATCH ME!
    you caught me!
    I love you!

now it's *your* turn

Invocation and Clowns, Dance of the Bareback Riders

eye of newt and heel of brandy
champagne wine and hashish candy
shock of love and touch of madness
demon's tear of final sadness
pulse of vision, blood of stone
kiss of witches, mandrake moan
fear of heaven, bread of dreams
Everything is what it seems

oh! the clowns! but they're beautiful
the ringmaster is clothed entirely in black owl feathers
except for his black suede boots and gauntlets
and his black and braided whip
He flies overhead, circling endlessly
while the clowns pretend to be angels
pretending to be clowns

and the bareback riders . . .
beautiful girls, naked except for silver boots and gloves
their long hair flowing behind them in a luminous wave
all of them, the ones pale and glowing as hot bridal satin
the ones dark as unknown waters   all of them
all of them ride horses white as mist with burning sapphire eyes
the horses canter and pace the figures of the dance
tails of seaspray   bodies cool as foam
the beautiful naked girls extend their arms
and weave serene enchantments as they dance
faster and faster
spinning their incandescent shadows into silver fog
that melts, dissolves, and burns
till all that's left transforms itself
into one glittering white and dawn wet rose
that the ringmaster
accepts in trembling hands

Freak Show and Finale

Expose yourself!
Show me your tattooed spine and star-encrusted tongue!
Admit your feral snarl, your bloody jaws
concede your nature and reveal your dreams!
        each beast contains its god, all gods are dreams
        all dreams are true

            LET THE BEAST WALK!!!!
        permit the dog to fly, allow the spider love

Are you the rainbow-headed child, the oracle of dream,
the witch of pain, the priest of tears, the door of love?

EXPOSE YOURSELF!
Are you the saint of lust, are you the beast that weeps?

EXPOSE YOURSELF!
Are you BOY 16 WEDS WOMAN 68 shaking with lust
Are you FATHER OF 3 SHOOTS SELF AND INFANT SON
Are you MANIAC BURNS LOVERS ALIVE
Are you UNKNOWN WOMAN LEAPS FROM BRIDGE
Are you TEEN-AGE GIRL FOUND CHAINED IN ROOM
Are you half-man half-woman, do you weigh six hundred
        pounds, can you
walk on your hands, write with your toes, dance on a
        tight-wire?

EXPOSE YOURSELF!

        ACCEPT THE CREATURE
        AND BEGIN THE DANCE!

Invocation for Maitreya

to invoke the divinity in man with the mutual gift of love
with love as animate and bright as death
the alchemical transfiguration of two separate entities
into one efflorescent deity made manifest in radiant human flesh
our bodies whirling through the cosmos, the kiss of heartbeats
the subtle cognizance of hand for hand, and tongue for tongue
the warm moist fabric of the body opening into star-shot rose flowers
the dewy cock effulgent as it bursts the star
sweet cunt-mouth of world serpent Ouroboros girding the universe
as it takes in its own eternal cock, and cock and cunt united
join the circle
moving through realms of flesh made fantasy and fantasy made flesh
love as a force that melts the skin so that our bodies join
one cell at a time
until there is nothing left but the radiant universe
the meteors of light flaming through wordless skies
until there is nothing left but the smell of love
but the taste of love, but the fact of love
until love lies dreaming in the crotch of god. . . .

Enlightenment Poem

we have all been brothers, hermaphroditic as oysters
bestowing our pearls carelessly

no one yet had invented ownership
nor guilt   nor time

we watched the seasons pass, we were as crystalline as snow
and melted gently into newer forms
as stars spun round our heads

we had not learned betrayal

our selves were pearls
irritants transmuted into luster
and offered   carelessly

our pearls became more precious and our sexes static
mutability grew a shell, we devised different languages
new words for new concepts, we invented alarm clocks
fences   loyalty

still . . . even now . . . making a feint at communion
        infinite perceptions
I remember
we have all been brothers
and offer   carelessly

Now Vision

we all lived (all) together in one (one) house sleeping in our various and separate rooms and I, I woke where I slept, in the arms of one who loved me, leaving four letter words undefined

oh yes I loved port wine warming my belly sweetening my mouth turning on my spirits even more I loved my pot curling incense up my head sliding ashes of laughter out my teeth (attar of roses) riding the vision night   I loved the sun sucking in in through my skin like a miser opening my mouth and my legs for the pretty sunshine loved the cold old fog loved the long wet rain   yet

my best and oldest friend in turning on the world forgot my name and left me hanging paranoid for twenty-seven minutes on an ill-used street with rescue an unasked stranger leading me beyond destruction cities below the earth   embracing me and we made love with each other sinking inexorably below the ground and waking as a bird, all hollow boned living together as we did the house began to change itself the day we gave up time my room turned golden

once we sat to dinner along the brown and broken table with twelve faces twenty-four hands forty-eight articulated limbs and knives and forks all making motions in the ritual air the masticating teeth saliva slippage down the long canal and peristalis little nodule muscles pushing in all the busy bellies I looked around my eyes at fork level and saw eleven sets of hands and one of golden paws taloned feral-clawed bloodstained I was afraid to look up and view what face or lack of one slipped down under the table and through the legs not looking backward and through the curtained doorway out

along the endless dusty hallway I dreamt my door opened into limbo I hung suspended there in nowhere while vampire bats twittered all the empty bed night with the moon burning my window and the wind at my door I could hear the earth turn and the stones crying in the fields and the ice crystals forming and shattering in my body veins my head was an unswept attic a ferris wheel of dust swinging through deserted fair grounds on a rainy night my eyes leaked cob-webs tomorrow I left my room singing chinese love songs out of the stretch of night

oh yes there were days and hours and I have walked this town until I have circled the universe   walking these streets back and forth and hiding in the bird sanctuary house we lived in and I walked down the hall and opened my door into turkish jazz and blew incense over the ceiling and lay down and wept for all the beautiful people now we all (all) lived in this house and there was Maru with her beautiful mis-sissippi bones and her dead baby staring thinly out the window and waiting to jump while her loving lover loved love somehow else and in another land   and there were more (passed out on the kitchen floor drunk again) there were bearded angels hugging scimitars there were unknown soldiers and glory diggers there were zen monks and lovely ladies there were sunflowers in the morning and passing the evening hours I drank blue vervain tea which tasted like bitter flowers like apri-cot kernels like witch fingers in this house sheltering many passers-by for this world is a bridge they say and it is a long time in crossing and we here ran a tea house with many exits.

oh the night hours the light hours the bright hours all the hours bundled up into each other made such a small package and all we really had

oh yes we are someone else now painting our eyes with the seasons I am a big angel bird squatting in a dark room watching my feathers grow they burst my skin infinitely   a blind seraph performing the Indian rope trick on a subway train

the season has changed the rain has washed away the earth and the flesh and the bones are whispering white secrets   this is the bridge this is the bridge and there is

no   way   back

Farewell to Fancy

Green-eyed, white limbed, the libra lady rides straight
down the wind. Nor does she safely sit and wait
for sweet serenity but opens wide for joy
and all devices of delirium she does employ.
Her sea-dawn eyes hold memories of antique Greece
when all the gods came down to kiss and laugh and twine
nor from that lovely loving did they cease
till all that once was human had become divine.

Let there be loving and let the joy run free
Think of this, lady, when you think of me.

Were–Poem

VISION OF BEASTS!
no man intransigent
but shields the animal within
were-wolf never died
but sits beside you
any time at all

and I have viewed the beast in man

last night I watched a poet glow white at the edges
and his face become that of a tiger

the beast is holy the man beast is holy
there are directions to go in that have never existed
the man is holy the tiger-lama invokes the voice of silence

EXPLOSIONS OF BEING !

the beast burns FIRE on the

HOLY balance waver FIRE

down the spine the man beast HOLY

in the beginning was HOLY
in the beginning was HOLY
in the beginning was HOLY

and there are existences beyond direction
HOLY

the mouth of the beast is filled with fire
and he speaks holy

and in the beginning was what flame-faced totality?

Rose/Vision

Permit me the concept of the rose
the perfumed labyrinth
that leads one petal at a time
into oblivion's heart

There are visions within the silence of the rose
Here in these velvet rooms accessible to dream
I open my eyes into darkness
until my vision/of itself/ignites the air
and I not only see but am all possibilities
of time and space and change
From which there is no place to hide, no
season of serenity, no solid ground
and Mother Chaos grips my trembling hand
and with *my* fingers tears the veil from her head
and shows me my own pale face
against the sparkling void
and I am bereft of explanations

I am at the turning of the labyrinth
and there is only one direction
and it surrounds me
and I am at the turning of the labyrinth
and there is only one way to go

The rose contains infinity, I hold the rose
and walk within the velvet tunnels of its dream
there is no way to stop or stand
and there is only one way to go

Age of Consent

I cannot be satisfied until I speak with angels
I require to behold the eye of god
to cast my own being into the cosmos as bait for miracles
to breathe air and spew visions
to unlock that door which stands already open and enter into the presence
of that which I cannot imagine

I require answers for which I have not yet learned the questions

I demand the access of enlightenment, the permutation into the miraculous
the presence of the unendurable light

perhaps in the same way that caterpillars demand their lepidoptera wings
or tadpoles demand their froghood
or the child of man demands his exit
from the safe warm womb

Lady/Poem

ladies with eyes limitless as angels
hover behind white windows
                pale windows
sending their minds over null-time landscapes
incandescent butterflies of breath

        THERE IS NO ROOF TO MY HEAVEN !

lady . . . lady . . . of iridescent dreaming
time is the gesture of your eyelash
                    dream of me,
                lady
my brain dances!

will we home to the right bodies, lady
                and will it matter

        THE RAINBOW!

                        it breaks   against my eye

        I, rainbow,
        do salute you
or will we giggle   and serve tea
            two hundred years too late

Stonedream

name me the sectors of reality, I am no longer sure
time is an invention of the phone company
the universe does not turn off in three minute spurts
clocks are a ploy of the devil

I have dreamed prophecies while wide-awake and found them true
        listen!   the honeybee dreams honey and I am awake at dawn
        remembering the corridors of dreams unsold
where was the beach on which I found this stone and from what mountain
was it washed what hillside knew it first did bee tracks dust its surface
was it a glacier gift from alpine tops the world has long forgot
        it fits my hand

Emerald Poem

there reaches a point without words
safe a point deep within the emerald
seabright washes over eyes and tongue

frozen the stonebirds fly soft among my fingers
their tiny beaks tapping snowflakes from my thumb
the color of emeralds
the solid becomes the liquid and I the greenbreather
I am at home among the nebulae
in the heart of the emerald
safe a point without words
one is one and I the green breather
I the gill singer
oh the liquid green flowers that the small birds carry!
they fade to lavender
on my tongue
they fade to lavender on my eyes
oh the stars that devour me in the heart of the emerald
safe in the flowers of the emerald
safe at the point without words

First They Slaughtered the Angels

I

First they slaughtered the angels
tying their thin white legs with wire cords
and
opening their silk throats with icy knives
They died fluttering their wings like chickens
and their immortal blood wet the burning earth

we watched from underground
from the gravestones, the crypts
chewing our bony fingers
and
shivering in our piss-stained winding sheets
The seraphs and the cherubim are gone
they have eaten them and cracked their bones for marrow
they have wiped their asses on angel feathers
and now they walk the rubbled streets with
eyes like fire pits

II

who finked on the angels?
who stole the holy grail and hocked it for a jug of wine?
who fucked up Gabriel's golden horn?
            was it an inside job?

who barbecued the lamb of god?
who flushed St. Peter's keys down the mouth of a
North Beach toilet?

who raped St. Mary with a plastic dildo stamped with the
Good Housekeeping seal of approval?
            was it an outside job?

where are our weapons?
where are our bludgeons, our flame throwers, our poison
gas, our hand grenades?
we fumble for our guns and our knees sprout credit cards,
we vomit canceled checks
standing spreadlegged with open sphincters weeping soap suds
from our radioactive eyes
and screaming
for the ultimate rifle
the messianic cannon
the paschal bomb

the bellies of women split open and children rip their
way out with bayonets
spitting blood in the eyes of blind midwives
before impaling themselves on their own swords

the penises of men are become blue steel machine guns,
they ejaculate bullets, they spread death as an orgasm

lovers roll in the bushes tearing at each other's genitals
with iron fingernails

fresh blood is served at health food bars in germ free
paper cups
gulped down by syphilitic club women
in papier-mâché masks
each one the same hand-painted face of Hamlet's mother
at the age of ten

we watch from underground
our eyes like periscopes
flinging our fingers to the dogs for candy bars
in an effort to still their barking
in an effort to keep the peace
in an effort to make friends and influence people

III

we have collapsed our collapsible bomb shelters
we have folded our folding life rafts
and at the count of twelve
they have all disintegrated into piles of rat shit
nourishing the growth of poison flowers
and venus pitcher plants

we huddle underground
hugging our porous chests with mildewed arms
listening to the slow blood drip from our severed veins
lifting the tops of our zippered skulls
to ventilate our brains
                    they have murdered our angels

we have sold our bodies and our hours to the curious
we have paid off our childhood in dishwashers and miltown
and rubbed salt upon our bleeding nerves
in the course of searching
                    and they have shit upon the open mouth of god
they have hung the saints in straightjackets and they have
tranquilized the prophets
they have denied both christ and cock
and diagnosed buddha as catatonic
they have emasculated the priests and the holy men and
censored even the words of love
          Lobotomy for every man!
and they have nominated a eunuch for president
          Lobotomy for the housewife!
          Lobotomy for the business man!
          Lobotomy for the nursery schools!
and they have murdered the angels

IV

now in the alleyways the androgynes gather swinging their
lepers' bells like censers as they prepare the ritual
rape of god
    the grease that shines their lips is the fat of angels
    the blood that cakes their claws is the blood of angels

they are gathering in the streets and playing dice with
angel eyes
they are casting the last lots of armageddon

V

now in the aftermath of morning
we are rolling away the stones from underground, from the caves
we have widened our peyote-visioned eyes
and rinsed our mouths with last night's wine
we have caulked the holes in our arms with dust and flung
libations at each other's feet

and we shall enter into the streets and walk among them and do battle
holding our lean and empty hands upraised
we shall pass among the strangers of the world like a
bitter wind

and our blood will melt iron
and our breath will melt steel
we shall stare face to face with naked eyes
and our tears will make earthquakes
and our wailing will cause mountains to rise and the sun to halt

THEY SHALL MURDER NO MORE ANGELS!
        not even us

Joy Song

My beloved wields his sex
like a hummingbird
poised on the delicate brink

What pleasure to be a honey plant
and
open wide

Eros/Poem

Praise be to young Eros who fucks all the girls!
Only the gods love with such generosity
sharing beatitude with all
Praise be to Eros! who loves only beauty
and finds it everywhere
Eros I have met you and your passing goddesses
wrapped in a haze of lovelust as true as any flower
that blooms its day and then is lost across the wind
I have seen your eyes lambent with delight
as you praised sweet Psyche's beauty with your loving tongue
and then have seen them sparkle with that same deep joy
as other tender ladies lay between your hands
Praise be to Eros! who can hoard no love
but spends it free as water in a golden sieve
sharing his own soft wanton grace
with all who let his presence enter in
faithless as flowers, fickle as the wind-borne butterfly
Praise be to Eros, child of the gods!
who loves only beauty   and finds it
everywhere

Hard Core Love

To Whom It Does Concern

Do you believe me when I say / you're beautiful
I stand here and look at you out of the vision of my eyes
and into the vision of your eyes and I see you and you're an animal
and I see you and you're divine and I see you and you're a divine animal
and you're beautiful
the divine is not separate from the beast; it is the total creature that
 transcends itself
the messiah that has been invoked is already here
you are that messiah waiting to be born again into awareness
you are beautiful; we are all beautiful
you are divine; we are all divine
divinity becomes apparent on its own recognition
accept the being that you are and illuminate yourself
by your own clear light

Love-Lust Poem

I want to fuck you
I want to fuck you all the parts and places
I want you all of me

all of me

my mouth is a wet pink cave
your tongue slides serpent in
stirring the inhabited depths
and then your body turns and
then your cock slides in my open mouth
velvety head against my soft pink lips
velvety head against my soft wet-velvet tongue
your cock /hard and strong/ grows stronger, throbs in my mouth
rubs against the wet slick walls, my fingers hold you
caress through the sweat damp hair
hold and caress your cock that slides in my mouth
I suck it in, all in, the sweet meat cock in my mouth and
your tongue slips wet and pointed and hot in my cunt
and my legs spread wide and wrap your head down into me

I am not sure where I leave off, where you begin
is there a difference, here in these soft permeable membranes?

you rise and lean over me
and plunge that spit-slick cock into my depth
your mouth is on mine
and the taste on your mouth is of me
and the taste on my mouth is of you
and moaning mouth into mouth

and moaning mouth into mouth

I want you to fuck me
I want you to fuck me all the parts and all the places
I want you all of me

all of me

I want this, I want our bodies sleek with sweat
whispering, biting, sucking
I want the goodness of it, the way it wraps around us
and pulls us incredibly together
I want to come and come and come
with your arms holding me tight against you
I want you to explode that hot spurt of pleasure inside me
and I want to lie there with you
smelling the good smell of fuck that's all over us
and you kiss me with that aching sweetness
and there is no end to love

Peyote Walk

I

VISION: that the barriers of time are arbitrary; that nothing is still

we, the giants of the river and universe, commencing the act of love, enclosing our bodies in each other's wilderness, vast hands caressing pinnacles of meat, tracing our titan thighs

one month we touch extremities
next year a kiss

the giant prick engorged began its downward stroke at years beginning into years end giant cunt (a) (slow) (sea) (clam) hips and rotundities earth-moving from month to month and promises of spring

orgasmic infinity
one (!) second long

EARTHQUAKE!
FLOOD! FLOOD! FLOOD!

huge pelvises shuddering
while worlds burn

2

VISION: that the barriers of form are arbitrary; nothing is still
now now now
moving
tangled my fingers tangle in
sticky life threads
moving
between my fingers

a geode, granite walled crystal universe
I see both sides at once
how easy why didn't I before

        I AM

part of the flow

    the lamp the fig and me
    we the redwoods
    us the walls and winds
      body mine?

  you?
MOTION

beingness my fingers t-
   angle

the only light our vital glow our radiance
turning to you your face becomes a skull
    MY SKULL!

protean the form encloses space and time
     moving

NOWNOWNOWNOWNOWNOWNOWNOW
   NOWNOWNOWNOW

  3

VISION: that yes
    (we) is (god)

Vision of the Skull of the Prophet

the bone is not white but yellowed; the skull blown thin
impaled in its entirety upon a staff of witch/wood

from the eyeholes there leaks a slow and steady stream
of minute iridescent crystals
descending like tears against the eroding bone
at the foot of the staff the ground is covered
with tiny crystalline flowers
that bloom only for an instant and then shatter
with the sound of light

in the moment of shattering the prophet-eye
views the universe entire
and dies again to dust

at that moment of sight
any being can share the total vision
any being whose eyes   at that incalculable instant
          are completely open

Poem for Tyrants

sentient beings are numberless—
I vow to enlighten them all
—The First Vow of Buddhism

it seems I must love even you
easier loving the pretty things
the children   the morning glories
easier   (as compassion grows)
to love the stranger

easy even to realize   (with compassion)
the pain and terror implicit in those
who treat the world around them
with such brutality   such hate

but oh   I am no christ
blessing my executioners
I am no buddha   no saint
nor have I that incandescent strength
of faith illuminated

yet   even so
you are a sentient being
breathing this air
even as I am a sentient being
breathing this air
seeking my own enlightenment
I must seek yours

if I had love enough
if I had faith enough
perhaps I could transcend your path
and alter even that

forgive me, then—
I cannot love you yet

The Farmer, the Sailor

"I've never seen the ocean . . ."
He stands there, looking out over the green of Wisconsin in August
(the spume of barley, the toss of oats, the drift of corn)
"It's a centennial farm—been in the family over a hundred years—
my grandpa broke the land—nobody else around here then—just him . . ."
It's an island, this place
the farmstead isolate in the high green
Out beyond the barn there's another building
the combine, the mower, rest there
and he strokes their orange bodies carefully
"You gotta have a feel for machinery. I always did. Do a lot of harvesting for people in this county, the next county, too. There was a bad hailstorm this year, almost went through the roof here, see?"
The dents show large in this thick metal roof. The building itself a ship's hull, joined precisely by his weathered hands.
"Broke all the windows in the house, that hail. Ruined the corn.
Planted a second crop though and we'll come out all right; if the weather holds fair."
He pats the combine gently
"No, I've never seen the ocean but I'd sure like to before I die.
Got a daughter out in San Francisco and my wife went out and visited her a year ago. She went right *in* the ocean, took off her shoes and lifted up her skirts and walked right in. Told me it was the prettiest thing she ever saw."
He stands there, the inland sailor, master mariner of the grassland
and his eye is blue with distance

Bus Ride

what savage beast would willfully consent to ride jammed haunch to haunch
with others of his kind
carried from spot to spot, glimpsing the passing world through
greasy rectangles of heavy glass
        oh god but we are civilized!
    observe the lady, matron-dominant by type
    she wears the uniform: mink coat, silk hat, a small corsage of pale
    Hawaiian blooms
        no use; old eve still wearing the skins of dead animals
            the genital organs of plants

I remember you, old lady, when you first decided you were such hot stuff,
prancing around on your hind legs with that phony apple in your teeth—
running on all fours when you thought no one was looking
        (I wonder, do you do that now—I can picture you in your
        bar-b-q back yard, stripped down to corset and falsies
        and whinnying at your neighbor's nubile sons with your
        finger up your flabby unsatisfied crotch while your
        de-balled houseman sits inside leafing through playboy
        and swallowing his spit)

again, you and your sisters do surround me, shining the plastic
seats with well-fed bottoms, your arms all crammed with
further goodies for your private delectation
were I that primal beast
I would have torn you joint by joint and saved your bones for
hard nights in the winter for my young to chew on but civilized
I sit in shame, guarding my own poor bones from such as you and
leaping from the bus to scurry home, intact
one time again

Anatomy Note

the hand is a flower
space moves the hand through areas of time the gesture
blooms and dies

Love Song for Snow White

in the hollow/of the garden/of the bed/in the crotch
/of the legs/of the tree
where we lie
time descends us like the moss   on an oaktree   on an ash
we grow younger   we grow tender
you and I

Bedsong for Her

tensions of Rosamond
        the lady fair
destroys herself as deft as any saint
and thirty times a virgin
        beds herself

O lullaby for seven peevish cats!

Poem for Peter

God's gentleman can do no wrong
nor right
he moves in grace
which holds no judgment

Three/Love Poem

I stood there with the two men
Kissing first one and then the other
Kissing first one and next the other
While the others laughed in envy and relief
That they didn't have to do it
And that it was being done

Melody for Married Men

I like to watch the young girls walk
swinging their hips and hair
swinging their hopes and dreams in magic circles
they never walk alone, but move in twos and threes
confiding audacities to each other
twitching their tails and giggling
while thirty year old men watch from their windows
drinking coffee with their wives and making fantasies
of Moslem heaven

Spring 61

country?   have lost our pride
as nationals   no man can die for billboards
as have for freedom
who froze his balls at Valley Forge
(14° below) pissed blood and wept in pain
(wept) wept a man willfully engaged
to fight for certain rights

My brother (34 years old)
drinks chocolate flavored metrecal
writing TV scripts
My lover (34 years old) catches fine fish
but cannot fill out forms
in triplicate
(Alaska is not for all of us)
he can barely buy brandy to blur his impotence
he is a man breaking his pride against

What Were Your Earnings Last Year
and
How Long Have You Lived At This Address
and
Are You Now

these men of Gloucester fought arm's length with whales
(the smell, they say, it never did wear off—
the reek of such huge dying)
why be   half safe

yesterday we went to the ocean and prised mussels
from low-tide rocks
cooked them with onion   carrots   celery seed
(delicious)
cut fingers healed in sea water

there is a pride in handknit sweaters
unknown
to knitting machines and
other robots

Gettysburg was not an outing
Bull Run, Appomattox, anywhere
and dance hall girls came high

Fort Sumter   Bunker Hill

THIS IS A NATIONAL MONUMENT

this African student, the other night
at a party
My people are dying, he said
yaws . . . fevers . . . things like that
I'd like to stay here, he said
direct plays . . .
I must go home and lead my people

Small Prayer for Falling Angels

too many of my friends are junkies
too many of my psychic kin tattoo invisible revelations on themselves
signing their manifestoes to etheric consciousness with little
hoofprint scars reaching from fingertip to fingertip
a gory religiosity akin to Kali's sacred necklace of fifty human heads

Kali-Ma, Kali-Mother; Kali-Ma, Kali-Mother
too many of my friends are running out of blood, their veins
are collapsing, it takes them half an hour to get a hit
their blood whispers through their bodies, singing its own death chant
in a voice of fire, in a voice of glaciers, in a voice of sand that blows
forever
over emptiness

Kali-Ma, remember the giving of life as well as the giving of death
Kali-Ma . . .
Kali-Ma, remember the desire is for enlightenment and not oblivion
Kali-Ma . . .
Kali-Ma, their bones are growing light; help them to fly
Kali-Ma, their eyes burn with the pain of fire; help them that they see
with clear sight
Kali-Ma, their blood sings death to them; remind them of life
that they be born once more
that they slide bloody through the gates of yes, that
they relax their hands nor try to stop the movement of the flowing now

too many of my friends have fallen into the white heat of the only flame
may they fly higher; may there be no end to flight

Naked I Have Known You

naked I have known you
I have watched your face open in the wet heat of love
your mouth of words become hunger and your tongue a
        delicate animal
I have known you

I have known you the skeleton exquisite walking the bright red flesh
cocooned in vegetable fiber and plastic and the skins of dead animals
moving with careful articulation through forest of concrete
eyeholes anxious at jungle intersections
the blare of sound an imprecation at finger-edge

the only way to walk is one foot on front of the other

FLY THEN GODDAM YOU!

witch-animal, scurrying to covens underground   rat brother
altar of subway trains   carrier of death capsule immaculate
V D
is watching you
oh junkie doorway god-love   the tremor of affliction beating your hand
against your other face
I have known you

wind eagle of high land I have seen your fingers elongate and burn
I have watched your groin flower
I have known you

naked I have known you I have devoured your head smashed through
mirror glass into dimensions uncontrollable I have found you
crystalline guts draped over/across my tongue and eyeballs and your
left hand in my stomach and I am digesting it

the most noticeable thing when falling into the sun is
the exquisite sensation of warmth

sun flower   sunflower dance floor   sunflower radio station
sunflower time bomb   sunflower dog kennel   sunflower
christmas tree   sunflower no trespassing   sunflower
white only   sunflower exit

naked I have know you hiding behind movie sets turning
yourself into holocaust   altar of windwheels
lobotomy dancer I have seen your eyelids nictate lace curtains
I have seen you eight feet high and skinny parading the city
dumps handweaving witch signs
and screaming

NAKED I HAVE SUNFLOWER YOU and the traffic
        backed up for miles
I have watched your face sunflower the eyeholes beds of
        hothouse dirt
and rare plants patterning your cheekbones mouth of sea
        anemone and I
have kissed it
redanimal I have greenplant you   altar of hockshops

and I have seen your face

Kirby/Poem

I have seen the blue eyes of the centaur
fiery with visions yet unprophesied
    the skull alchemic furnace of the man
        the mind/serpent devouring
        the marrow of the nether bones

    VISION VISION
    DREAM DESCRIBABLE
PENULTIMATE PROPHECY OF THE BLUE-FLAME LOVE/DEATH

Peering beyond and through the eye apertures
I see your skull a geode
Stone shelled kaleidoscope of light

    Within the interior labyrinth of the mind
    the crystal slowly blooms
    transmuting the melted dross
    the soft tissues and decaying bones

THE BEING ITSELF IS THE ONLY SUFFICIENT FUEL

Centaur I have known you before me on the zodiac
nudging my heels with your prophetic arrow

Bone bow bone arrow
gut strung
and with your own untidy guts
Time was I knew you thick with meat
and steady with your years

This day I see your arrow tremble in the sky

Junk/Angel

I have seen the junkie angel winging his devious path over cities
his greenblack pinions parting the air with the sound of fog
I have seen him plummet to earth, folding
his feathered bat wings against his narrow flesh
pausing to share the orisons of some ecstatic acolyte
The bone shines through his face
and he exudes the rainbow odor of corruption
his eyes are spirals of green radioactive mist
luminous even in sunlight   even at noon
his footstep is precise, his glance is tender
he has no mouth nor any other feature
but whirling eyes above the glaring faceless face
he never speaks and always understands he answers no one
Radiant with a black green radiance
he extends his hollow fingered hands
blessing   blessing   blessing
his ichorous hollow fingers caressing the shadow of the man
with love and avarice
and Then unfurls his wings and rides the sky like an
enormous Christian bat   and voiceless
flies behind the sun

Blues for Sister Sally

I

moon-faced baby with cocaine arms
nineteen summers
nineteen lovers

novice of the junkie angel
lay sister of mankind penitent
sister in marijuana
sister in hashish
sister in morphine

against the bathroom grimy sink
pumping her arms full of life
(holy holy)
she bears the stigma (holy holy) of the raving christ
(holy holy)
holy needle
holy powder
holy vein

dear miss lovelorn: my sister makes it with a hunk
of glass do you think this is normal miss lovelorn

I DEMAND AN ANSWER!

II

weep
for my sister she walks with open veins
leaving her blood in the sewers of your cities
from east coast
to west coast
to nowhere

how shall we canonize our sister who is not quite dead
who fornicates with strangers
who masturbates with needles
who is afraid of the dark and wears her long hair soft and black
against her bloodless face

III

midnight and the room dream-green and hazy
we are all part of the collage

brother and sister, she leans against the wall
and he, slipping the needle in her painless arm

pale fingers (with love) against the pale arm

IV

children our afternoon is soft, we lean against each other

our stash is in our elbows
our fix is in our heads
god is a junkie and he has sold salvation
for a week's supply

Morning Song

Walking in the sweet stale smell of his fond wife's armpit George Vardo remembered realized and regretted the passage of his life, visualizing it as some peculiar bird flapping away past a dreary broad-beamed ferry boat. Where, when, how, he couldn't recall, hadn't noticed, didn't know, only the goneness of it and here he was himself again after an absence of unknowable time.

Eyes shut as an unborn bird he lay unmoving and examined the presence of his wife. wife. WIFE. wiFe. wife. She smelled of moderate talcum powder and pale perfume. Saturday movie theaters. Shoe sweat and popcorn. Undertones of good toast and a rhyme of bacon.

She existed.

Somewhere directly beside him, adjoining his right flank and chest and outflung arm lay a woman. his. wife.

His arm? He flexed the fingers carefully. His arm.

Below him the bed sagged with familiarity. Unyoung. There had been a bed once with gilded frame and orchid colored sheets. great vistas of bedliness. tense springs and eager linen. This bed? NO! never this bed. had been young . . . ever? woven knitted hammered nailed glued and varnish smelling randy legged had sat smug waiting the floor of a department store bounced on by newlyweds with springly heart in price-tag mouth virgin having petted touched felt poked but never DONE THAT THING and sold and carted off and learned the secrets of the night has come to THIS that bed?

He let the hairs on his legs reach out and brush the sheets. They felt gray used until they confided themselves to his body like beaten dogs, cringing spiritless sheets.

Wife? His hand was afraid to reach and touch, he flared his nostrils in exploration.

There had been a woman mountain size whom he had wanted with fervid eagerness aching to dive in and excavate, darkest africa with pick and shovel, race up steaming canals, slide all the way up her and out her startled mouth running and making mountain yodels of exhilaration and you can't catch me.

Anxious he felt the balance of the bed and it lay even weight for weight and let his breath come out a little gust of wind. Then not the little girl half-elf come sliding other-world into his hands one street-loose evening when he had been heavy-footed with hunger and hardly looking up and she so soft and small made streetlights into stars.

a little gust of sigh catching his heart he snored ashamed and then ashamed of shame let sighs be sighs.

He reached himself out and his wife rose to him like bread dough, she still asleep and he cringed back a fractured snail and rolling out of bed and naked scurrying through the dusty floor and out the room and never looking once.

And then beyond the door he stood within a narrow hall and dressed himself in black and with a red rose in his hand went out into the real world.

and opened up his eyes.

The street was long enough and he was wide enough and George Vardo woke up in the familiar warmth of his wife's body and they performed an act of fornication and shared nothing for breakfast and George dressed himself and went to work

feeling. somewhere.

a faint disturbing sense of loss.

Telephone from a Madhouse

the way it happens, I'm sitting here in this semi-secure four-walled building
there is the cool texture of a wooden floor under my naked feet
and I'm drinking black coffee
from a pretty rice bowl that curves my hands
when the phone rings
and when I lift that dark plastic instrument and put it to my
ear, put it to my carelessly hello-ing mouth
this voice from a million miles away, from a treeless plain,
from a gray wet dank abyss
comes out to me
Are you there? it says, the anxiety of it cutting my calm like a
spiritual buzz saw
Are you there? Are you *really* there? Sometimes I can't believe
you exist, are you there, are you there, really there?
Yes, I murmur, yes yes yes, gripping at the floor with my bare
brown toes, rubbing my sweaty fingers against the wall
Yes, I murmur, yes yes yes   counterpoint to the soft and
desperate tears that drip over the phone at me
Yes, I say firmly, snapping my voice like a lion whip, I'm here
I'm here I REALLY EXIST
and my hands wandering the hall, rubbing my tense muscled
thigh, spreading themselves before my analytic eyes
Yes, I murmur, yes, yes, yes

Later I pass behind the polite and sterile madhouse walls
flashing my visitor look at the fish-eyed nurses
and padding down the barren corridor to room on the left
number seven
where the voice lies waiting
tangled in soiled bedclothes her   old woman slow
feral eyes break at me   shuffle walking
among the tears the   up and down
darkened room she   the hall
leans up stares at   all the time
me arrowing my soul   all the time

the voice sobs at me
YOU CAME   oh i
can't go on i can't
i don't want to live
any more   and tears
blossom reblossom
man-eating flowers out of
the puffy gray-green eye
sockets they eat up her
swollen face WHAT AM I
GOING TO DO
I wiggle up onto the thin
and high and narrow bed
utterly wordless I reach
out arm around the pale
body in split back
hospital sackcloth and
head against my shoulder
she SCREAMS
and nurse ambulances up
sirening
as I whisper it's all right
trying to push the words
out through my fingers
on her shaky back and
fixing nurse with
glaring eyes until she
drifts away in
starched disorder
showering me with
distrust but
going
I whisper whisper it's
all right   until the
sobbing softens and

shuffle up
and down the
corridor
up and down
up and down

one foot drags

visitors pass by
furtively
wearing outdoor
faces and peering
into the rooms
as if they were
keyholes

her sad head lifts
and questions me
again
it *is* all right I
whisper and
thank you   she
whispers back
but is it?   and
I am speechless
pull out one small
gray pigeon feather
I found lying on
the steps of
the hospital
and offer it
she takes and
strokes it, nodding
her head
pigeons are real it
seems
thank you she whispers
again   and
we keep nodding
two windy figures
in a Chinese gale
Are you all right
she asks
It's a beautiful day I
answer the sun is
blooming the flower I
found roses on the
sidewalk
in North Beach
(nodding)
we had a party last

the room is
small the walls
are enema yellow
the shade is down
the light is off
it could be any
hour in the world

GODDAM IT   you
think I'll stand
for this well I
won't I'll show
you all you bloody
jackasses   screams
next door

old woman up and
down the corridor
all the time
all the time

face peers in the
room and
goes
away

night I had tea cakes
for lunch how are
you
Terrible, she nods
terrible
i don't think i'll
ever get well
i'm afraid
they want me to get
out of bed
and i can't
i smell bad
the world is
disintegrating and
i don't have
anything to hold
on to

and she is trembling
in the terrible wind
the tears are
gobbling her eyelids
nobody will ever
love me she sighs
i am afraid   i am
afraid of everything
terrible she nods
terrible
I kiss her tears like
january sleet touch
my mouth and
I go away

up and down
up and down

right foot drags

HELP a voice
calls piteously
help   help
help

help

VISITING HOURS

ARE NOW

OVER

In Transit

Question: Locate the center of infinity
Answer: Anywhere

IT   NEVER STOPS   MOVING!

The ceaseless alchemical permutation, gold into history,
rain into strawberries, strawberries into my bloodstream,
my blood into flowering dreams

the dream into absolute perception, into coruscating visions of
THIS IS WHERE IT IS BA–BY into
infinity

It is necessary to search the spirit through the light of one's
own bioluminescence

THERE IS NO SUCH THING AS STANDING STILL

The balance is that of a gyroscope, motion existing within motion
the balance of a bird listening to its heartbeat
wings poised against the currents of the air, eyes tracing the
turning of the earth, the planet circling the sun, the sun spinning
its golden path in the universe, and the universe breeding life and
death in infinity

and the bird hangs halfway up the sky
infinite motion   at rest   within infinite motion

LET IT GO!

"Whatever you see that is beautiful
        don't hang on to it
whatever you see that is terrible
        don't hang on to it"

LET IT GO!

The balance is that of sunlight on water
the sunlight moving as the earth turns, the water
following its gravity path into eventual raindrops
and home to another river
the sunlight-and-water being one and together for the
duration
of their parallel flow

there is no way to stop water
if you lock it up it will evaporate and reach the clouds
anyhow
there is no way to stop the sun
it holds its own galactic balance and moves
according to the nebulae of outer space

LET IT GO!

IT NEVER STOPS MOVING

there is movement within a mountain
a rock, a thought, a flower, a light bulb,
a cat, a star, a rice bowl, an arrow

LET IT GO!

IT NEVER STOPS MOVING

there is no such thing as standing still
the direction of motion is frequently a matter of choice
when you try to stop other things from moving
you give yourself an impetus toward backwards motion

LET IT GO!

Most of the time
        you will be the *it*
being let go of

In the Comics

last night I saw the holy trinity
        Superman, Batman, and Robin
they were shooting it up in my bathroom
when I came home from a hard day's dreaming
OH   POP!   OH   ZAP!
Superman alone did up 700 ccs of POW!

Later we traded secrets
I told them nothing and they told me all

        there are only ten real people left outside the comics
        everyone else is a Martian
                or a hero
        or a robot programmed to think he is a hero
                    or you

                WHAM! well pop my zowie, dad, who would have dreamt
                that Superman was really the Panchan Lama, and sitting
                right next to me here at school!

Captain Marvel is your mother

                    (I suppose you wonder why I came to you in
                    the garb of an Egyptian temple dancer of
                    nearly two thousand years ago)

        POW! WHAMMMMMM! OH   ZOWIE   ZOWIE   ZOWIE!

        Batman makes it with Robin
        Robin makes it with eagles
        Superman never does

        BAM! BAM! THUD! CRAAAACK!

(to others it looks as if the positioning of her arms
is part of a dance but to me her arms are signaling
information in semaphore)

Superman is a Martian in drag! ZOOOOOOM!
Wonder Woman is Superman in drag! ZIIIIP!

DRAG! DRAG! DRAG!   ZIP! ZIP! ZIP!

(helpless in the clutches of the awesome
monster from another time Batman rolled
up his sleeve and shot up three thousand
ccs of WHAM!)

(I weigh only ninety-eight pounds—yet I can
paralyze a 200 pound attacker with just a finger—
because I know   VAZAAAAAAAAAAP!)

oh SCRUUUUNCH, baby, we can't go on this way any longer,
there must be a way out of this costume!

KA—WHAMPF!

CRANNNNNNNG!   BLAM! BLAM! BLAM!

Dad! Superman stands for law, justice, and order!
Why is he acting like a tyrant?

Pffffff! Click! Hmmmmmmmmm!

Search on! Search all you want! The only way
you'll ever find it is with the help of these
magic mushrooms!

BAM! BAM!

THUD!

Time's running out fast! If only the clock
would stop ticking . . .

ZIP! POW! WOWIE!

then I'm no longer a super-hero but
just another broken down old has-been

WE ARE ALL EQUALLY INVINCIBLE!

WOW! WOW! WOOOOOOOW!

Horoscope

!FIRE!

this is the day all library books become due

!FIRE!

this is the day the sewers break and the gas is shut off

!FIRE!

this is the ohglorygod listen to the song of the white-crowned
sparrow outside my narrow citystreet window outside
my narrow night and heartache

!FIRE!

you are kind, obedient, thoughtful, and a pederast

!FIRE!

Orphan Annie has a controlled habit
so does her dog

!FIRE!

you are going on a long trip
you are not going on a long trip
you are going to get busted by a spaghetti-eating cop and sentenced
to nine years in a tract house scrawling HELP on the windows with
a broken enema tube

!FIRE!

you are going to eat a tall dark man

!FIRE!

(how many times have I told you to put a
newspaper under your feet when you lie down
on the couch I mean after all you could show
a little consideration)

!FIRE!

(I'd buy your painting but the color just
doesn't go with my new living room set do
you have one with more red in it??)

!FIRE!

your fly is unzipped

!FIRE!

wouldn't you be happier with your own people

!FIRE!

there is no forecast for tomorrow

!FIIIIIIIIIIIIIIIIIIIIRE!

Poem for Perverts

Come be my leather love!
and hand in glove we'll play our own amazing games
behind locked doors and silent window shades

But she's exquisite!
Six and a half inch high black patent leather boots
that lace up tightly to the tender crotch, a brass and
leather belt of chastity, a French-made corset that
laces sixteen inches small, black leather gloves from
fingernail to armpit (so tight it took an hour to ease
them on), and best of all, a featureless black leather
hood fitting over the entire head and gathered snugly
at the neck permitting (exquisite!) only desperate
painful breathing and no movement whatsoever

Be mine! Be mine!
I'll buy you iron fetters for your tiny wrists!

The Fat Man, completely naked except for black
leather gloves, made a gesture and they removed the
hood leaving only a thick blindfold. They forced her to
her knees in front of him and he put his gloved hands
on her head and giggled softly as he pushed it where
he wanted it. There was nothing she could do except obey.

I'll buy you manacles and thongs
and lash you trembling to the chairs
I'll lead you at midnight on a dog chain
to secret parties where Lady Olga demands *discipline*
and even I am subject to her whims

Exotic ladies!
Members of CLUB UNUSUAL!
Heroines of the spanking brigade
Heroes in lace-trimmed silken underwear, subjected to
UNSPEAKABLE INDIGNITIES!

Virgins of thirty-six with elongated tongues and clawlike nails
Affectionate young man, accustomed to discipline and fond of frolic
Will cook and clean, desires only good home and a
STERN MISTRESS
UNSPEAKABLE INDIGNITIES!

Come be my bondage queen!
We'll meet on Friday afternoons and play
"Who'll Wield the Whip" and "Hide the Dildo"
you'll count to ten and find yourself in any one of seventy predicaments

Bound To Please!

The bride wore black leather and carried a neat
bouquet of riding whips; the groom donned a French
maid's costume and was given away by Madame
Tyrant of the well-known Tyrant Boarding Academy.
The nuptials were celebrated by the Fat Man,
who accepted the caudal kiss from all participants
at the close of the ceremonies.

Love, he whispered. Love is my whip
and etched his ardor on her slender back

The blood wreathed down like roses!
until she wept for joy who also wept for pain

Behold the fantasy of man gone civilized!
No naked brute could dream these delicate deceits

“Be mean to me,” he begged
“No,” she said, “I won’t, I won’t do it”
“Ah,” he sighed ecstatically,
“I knew that you’d be mean”

“Lick it!” demanded Madame Olga, and Poor Francine complied, the tears running down her tender cheeks

“Lick it!” demanded the Fat Man, and Poor Evelyn obeyed.
She was chained on hands and knees but she lifted her head obediently, her blue eyes overflowing with tears

“Lick it!” ordered Nina, the French Maid, and Poor Harry did as she said, having learned the folly of rebellion at the cruel hands of Madame Tyrant

Lick it! Adore the booted foot, the gloved hand, the whip, the rod, the Agony Pear, the manacles, the chains, the Witches’ Cradle, and the spanking board!
There is no way out, each door a further entrance to new indignities and epicurean conceits of anguish impossible to dream on, the carnivorous bloom of flowering neurosis gone to synthetic seed.
There are no exits in Bondageland, there is no way back!

Exquisite! breathed the Fat Man
He adjusted his pallid bulk delicately
and mounted the blue-eyed corpse

III.

Poems from Three Penny Press Chapbooks

(1959)

All I have in the world
Dark brown hair and a restless mind
I can feel the earthquakes underneath my feet
    waiting to explode, to erupt, to go boom!
I am waiting,
I am squatting in the middle of my floor
    Buddha-postured, lily-livered,
        I am getting rather bored
I am tired of my navel, as exquisite as it is
And the floor is getting harder,
        getting harder all the time
I am waiting for explosions,
        for vast tremors of the earth
        smithereens and smashings,
        constellations going wild
I am bored with sitting wisely,
        I am tired of being calm
I would like to sit on mountain tops
        and watch the lava flow
    and aid in flinging boulders
        at the commoners below
I would like to burn the house down
    and move to somewhere else
Or walk the streets at midnight,
    laughing madly to myself
Take my car and run down people
    who are smugly marching home
    with their grubby bags of pickles
        held beside them—
And shibboleths and syllogisms,
        Sunday schools and soap,
    wouldn't mean a single bloody thing,
                not a thing,
I'm getting sick of lollypops,
        the nausea of the age
Sitting smugly, sitting wisely,
    so remotely all alone

(But can navel-gazing quite replace
a well-played slide trombone?)
I'll implode myself, enfold myself,
a single blood-shot eye
Watching oh so sadly as the fragments all drift by

For I'm getting rather tired and
I'm getting rather bored

And if something doesn't happen
I'll go

stark

staring

BOOM!

Apogee

Mumble, mumble, I am God
I am president of the United States of confusion,
contusion, collusion, and schmoozin'
Mumble, mumble, I am God
I am a hundred and ten feet tall
My eyes peer clear to the bottom of the sea
Mumble, mumble, I am God
My head is higher than my feet
My bones are strong, my flesh is sweet
I beat my daddy with a boogie beat
Mumble, mumble, I am God
I am God, and God's almighty
Little girls are often flighty
Grandpa wears a pin-striped nighty
Mumble, mumble, shot my wad.

Clearly beloved, we are huddled here together
because
There is no place else to go

On some streets they even fence the trees,
        guarding their sooty bodies behind
        sooty iron palisades

In the country
        they fence bulls and chickens and
        woe betide him who here forgets to
            leash his dog

Nightingales sing at noon
        and we are locked in cafeterias,
        part of an endless line
        of slop-stuffers

Somebody cleans the sewers every hour of the day
But museums close in the afternoon

Let me roll myself in the pleasures of love,
        let me wear rings on my toes,
                                flowers in my hair,
        let me breathe perfume, and
        run through dirt barefoot

Even so beloved, even so
There is no way out of here

We are locked in the cage and somebody
out there
has thrown away the key.

1. Hey, hey, I have a universe to share with you
It wonders me, this pocket full of words

Hey, hey, I'll give you blood to drink
My own, your own, the reddest wine I know

Nibbling, munching,
    we'll gnaw out all the sweet flesh

Leaving our strong and silver skeletons
    Little bones locking

To lean in tenderness
    while the breezes blow little songs
        Through our ribs

2. All our feet are tired
    let us kiss (soft-lipped) the tender toes
    behind the knees,
    the shoulders,
    finger-tips and mouth
    To mouth
Sucking our breath,
We will lie and die in sweetness
Gasping, grasping death

3. Naked to naked till even the smallest bones
Are crunched for marrow
Look to the phoenix
And from this pile
    of oh-so-tired dust
I see the first faint stirring
        of a golden wing.

Home is where you find it.
Find is where you home it.
It is where you.

The hot wind blows and
  I wish I could blow with it
Head under heels and completely

How can I trust you
  when your eyes are shuttered peepholes

Open your eyes to me
  so I can see you
  so I can stay

Catch me before I run away
  before I'm lost

My courage has no substance and
My heart turns winter at
  the first faint touch of frost

Hungry as a sulky child nothing suits me
I have no taste for meat nor cake nor wine
    but my belly rumbles
Sitting on the curbstones of the world
    We are the isolate, the always watching
Perceiving in each beginning
    the seeds of its end
Planting them ourselves
    lest we be caught unaware

I gave you all the rains
    that walk in the night
All the winds,
    and the weepings,
        and the whispers.

Like I was both here and here simultaneously;
    hearing with the edges of my ear,
    rolling the air on my tongue
        before swallowing
    like a gray-haired wine taster.

Feeling the soft heaviness of my eyelids.

I have chosen for my guide the gray wind
    the old wind, the cold wind
    that nibbles the edges of the world
All my pockets have holes in the bottoms
    and everything I own slides away . . .
        sooner or later

I gave my love a cherry
    and they drowned it in Kentucky bourbon
I gave my love a chicken and they rung its neck
    and roasted it, munching the bones like savages
I gave my love a ring and they hocked it
I gave my love a baby and they killed it

I took a deep breath and climbed a tall tree
    to look clearly at the world
As I settled myself in the high branches
    they chopped it down and
    I was back among the multitude
I filled my pockets with nothing and started again
me and the gray wind
the gray wind and I
Forever and never amen

I have fallen in love with the wind

I know I can't catch it

but it plays such a pretty tune
    through the holes in my head

That I have fallen in love.

I thought you were a man
Solid to rock against warm in the cool of the night

When I reached for you
    you dissolved in my hand like ashes
Blowing away on the wind

What could I do but resolve into a swallow
Flying southward after summer

The love I had for you, baby
    Was like a big, fat, glassy jewel
Shiny like snow in the morning
        And I was a goddamn fool.

I walked in with my eyes wide open
    Like a sheep that can't wait to be led
I had it made, I was living
    Love, like a hole in the head.

Loving and love being the reason behind it all
I woke up one Tuesday morning
Determined to
The streets were full
    but the faces were empty
And I stood there like a pilgrim
Dripping love from my hands
    to the cold gray sidewalk
I walked till I reached a corner
    full of four choices
None of them was mine,
    so I sat on the curbstone and waited
I didn't know it but I was waiting for you
And when you got there I knew it all
Oh, when I met you
    your only shoes had holes in the bottoms,
And when we went home together
The sheets were gray on your bed
And when I left saying I'd be back tomorrow
I forgot that tomorrow is a never-ending word

When I returned they had torn down the building
    and forgotten your name even I
But loving being the first and only question
And the first and only answer
I turned to the streets like a pilgrim
And sat down at the corner
    knowing you'd pass by
    some time or other
And sitting there I and love
    turning the air around me
    all golden as summer time ends

Mountains and cities and pitfalls and
people and crawling past the meridians,
the tropics,
the degrees of lat and long,
the poles and the oceans,
the bitter seas of tears,
the winter time of love,
the carnival of sleep.

My beloved has a hundred faces and none of them are mine. I have walked up and down on the slanted streets and I have never met a unicorn. I have passed the doorways built of wood and the doorways built of stone. People wait upon the corners but they do not wait for me and I pass by them. I have looked in the shop windows and I have never seen a gold-set miniature that was my love. I have found papers on the street and when I read them they told me nothing. I have walked the docks and seen the tall ships arrive and depart but I did not join the throngs upon them. I have seen the blunt-nosed barges sail past me on the river. I have gone into the department stores and when I asked them, they had no rubies for a quarter. I have sat on park benches in the springtime and the fall. Old men walked by but they offered me no wisdom and the children passed on roller-skates. I have gone into the eating-places and found no roses on my plate. I have walked the streets at midnight and at dawn and my feet have never turned to silver.

Sometimes I wonder if they ever will.

My love gave me an orange tree
which would not bear
I planted it in my belly
and laid myself down in the soft dark earth
lapping myself with leaves like a coverlet
But our tree bore no fruit
and its roots spread through my body
and pinned me to the barren ground.

I love you.
Simpler than that
      I can not be.

Oh, my beloved . . .
Oh my long-eyed, whispering beloved . . .
The night is long and far too long for me
And the image of the moon
hangs on my wall.

The walls are thin around me
and I can feel the night

Lapping at my doorstep with a pointed tongue.

Our morning is afternoon,
    and we emerge into twilight.

Bedtime is daytime,
    and we come into bloom
        after midnight.

Ours are the telephones
    that ring like alarm clocks
        at one o'clock
        at noon.

Like seasonless fowl we migrate . . .
    from East Coast to West Coast
    and back and forth again,
        for a job,
        for a friend,
        for a change,
        for a kick.

Apartments with mobiles
        and heavy curtains.

Guitar players.
    Drummers
        and all the other.

Unwashed dishes.

Books from
    science fiction to
    thomasmccullers sterneeliotcummingsmiller
    and all the rest,
    several stolen from your local library.

Records in jazz and
    folksong hindemith and
    selections from the congo on
        drum bones
        dog whistle
            grunts
            screams and
            tongue clicks.

Blue jeans and labels from Saks.
                Sandals.

Your bed is my bed,
        loan me your shirt?

Borrow your shower,
        cock-a-dood le prrrrrt

A Passing Dragon

In the beginning . . .
There was . . .
Nothing . . .
Everything . . .
Sometimes . . .
Often . . .
And me
So I started on the narrow road that led nowhere
Screaming and howling and yelling, but I couldn't stay
where I was because that was disappearing rapidly
So I jumped on the treadmill
catching a ham on rye without mustard and a typewriter
and a pair of rubber overshoes that I couldn't stand
from the first moment I saw them
Ten minutes or maybe it was ten years later I nearly
fell off into a passing dragon's passing mouth
But a taxicab honked and saved me
I climbed back on the straight-and-narrow narrow
And continued serenely by the wild parties and the wild
women and the wild dogs and the wild wild wild
And finally I reached the end of the road
And there I was
Nowhere

Pigeons always spell New York to me
Their fat pigeon asses waddling
down concrete streets,
hanging off window sills,
taking a casual shit on
some great statesman's stony face.

And at the edge of the town,
Brooklyn and the Bronx,
where the subway comes up for air
like a drowning swimmer

The pigeons gather on the rails,
pecking at lost salted peanuts
and exchanging chittering gossip

Erupting upward like a feathering elevator
when the trains rumble into view.

Hollywood is no place for a decent bird
scratching at palm trees and orange peels.
Like a knight crusader,
I am moved to start a trek to the Holy Land
Thousands of penitent pigeons marching across country
Through the corn lands
and the wheat lands,
the steel towns
and
the mill towns
Hoboing their way on the roofs of freight cars,
catching a lift on the tops of trucks
Chattering their way to the
dirty sidewalks and the tall buildings

Pigeons always spell New York to me.

Slipping into my heart as once
    you slipped between my legs . . .

I never knew you, but I'll love you now
Now that you're dead and
    carrion birds are sucking at your mouth

You would stay up all night,
        afraid to sleep
Clutching at the hours between
        the dark and dawn
    as if each one was the gold ring
    on your private merry-go-round.

How right you were!
for sleep has stolen every second of your soul
    and left you lying there,
        a feast for ants,
        a storehouse of decay,
    with bony hollows
    where once your eyes did burn.

The brilliant prisms of your mind have stilled
    and where they played,
      now sharp-tongued insects
      lap their daily bread.

Oh, how you laughed beside the sea,
      a prisoner of words,
    reaching with your soul
    as babies reach their hands

You kissed me and
    your mouth was full of hunger
    for which no food was made

I think you starved to death
    although they put up signs
    that read in big black letters,
            PLAGUE.

(They think I'm mad, you told me once.
I was afraid to answer,
    with the same hush that stilled barbarians
    as they passed a waiting sacrifice)

I never knew you,
    but I'll weave a basket of your bones
        and hide it in the fire,

        lying there naked,

waiting
for dawn
to start
my walk
        across the earth.

Take one giant step, lady

    potatoes five cents a pound,
        no bus tokens accepted,
    subways built of iron and
    churches built of steel

    stealing is sinful, delightful,
            langorous, lovely and
    two lumps of sugar and
    two lumps of tea   HELP!

One step forward and one step back

Living is loving is lovely is sticky warm hot

Mezzanine: contraceptives, alligators,
back-scratchers and ladies
lingerie.

Watch your step

Please

Look, ma, I'm flying!

No hands

no feet

no nothing

Bye.

Such a tomcat then
    sitting there preening his belly fur
White teeth gleaming through his whiskers
And his pale eyes insatiate
(So infuriating to a she-cat
Fence walking the world
    to be beckoned
    and rolled
    and left to meander critically on)

Leg cocked high he polishes his penis and
    moves on

There is a hole in my heart,
all the love is dripping out
and the winds of summer
have forgotten how to
          spell my name

The frost grows heavy on my eyelids,
      my fingers have no gloves,
            my body has no skin

I am a jellyfish in a world of iron pokers
A child will scoop me up and take me home,
      preserve me in a jar of alcohol,
      put my body on a spare-room shelf

                                    And I
          will never see the sun again.

This is my world,
the world of earliest morning

When I drive the streets like God
in a steel-bound car

Heading homeward into the wild-eyed sunrise,
the glowing dawn.

These are my streets
I love them

The empty streets,
the heavy-lidded windows
peering blindly at nothing
The stolidly blinking signals,
hoarding strength for later.

The hopeless neon begging me to
eat here,
buy this,
remember us
in time of need

Knowing so well I'll never
eat here,
buy this,
or remember.

Like a shooting star a car passes by,
appears, and is gone,
Leaving only the faintest awareness
to pervade my morning

That I am not quite alone

And the stragglers,
    the last pale remnants of the night people
And the pale vanguard of the day,
    the earliest sewer cleaners,
    the most prompt bus drivers

And me,
    First of the first,
    The last of the last

I rocket homeward to dive into bed,
    wrapping the sheets around my head as
    morning
        comes knocking
            at my window.

The Twenty Nine Hungers of God

Joe T. Emmons woke up one morning and the first hunger was orange juice and coffee with eggs and stuff stacked in-between. And the second hunger was sunlight which was like whipped cream when he walked through it, breasting the air like the only swimmer in a blue-green ocean.

There was loneliness, which he found at 4 a.m. on a subway and noon in a cafeteria; peace, which he found in a nudist camp; faith, when a child yelled "catch me!" and jumped;

And he fucked and he fucked and he fucked and he fucked, pausing only for a hot dog which satisfied two hungers at once since it included self-immolation.

The last hunger was for the unattainable and he shattered into a thousand glittering fragments when a bomb appeared singing just the right note.

You are like a lion
    crashing the bars of your cage

And I am like an idiot
Trying to stay you
                    with
                     peanuts.

You there! You with the loneliness
poking through the corners of your eyes.
I have met you once before, I think.

On a street corner in the middle of a city
with the neon rippling over soot-stained walls
and the crowd walking backwards and forward.

With a band blaring its way out of a
red-doored night club and the
sidewalk glittering mica
where the street lamps hit.

You were standing there with the wind
curling around your ears,
staring at a window filled with
tinkertoys and imitation diamonds.

Or was it later, maybe, in a silent street
where blank windows winked
their yellow-lace eyelids at each other.

Your conversation, friend,
Is like a page of written Hebrew:
    There are no vowels in it.

Vowels rhymes with bowels,
    And there are no guts in you.

IV.

Poems from Little Magazines and Broadsides

(1960–2004)

Speaking of . . .

It all began when Bodhidharma appeared floating in mid-air
simultaneously over
Times Square
            the Golden Gate Bridge
                              and Metro-Goldwyn-Mayer
in each case attended by seventeen lingam-oriented nuns playing
Dixieland on B♭ harmonicas
every taxi in sight blinked its headlights reverently
and the horns blew for one and one-half solid hours
deafening all bubble gum chewers
                instantly

in San Francisco the bhikkus and the stockbrokers two-stepped
out of the hills
pelting the cheering crowds with chocolate covered deximils
and yellow roses

in New York everyone came out of the subways—
there were faces there that hadn't seen daylight in years
and dissolved at once under the strain

the trolls, the elephants, and the Polish bagpipers' union
danced the hora in Central Park
while little children on roller skates distributed reefers
and the French navy took over the Staten Island ferry
sailed it to Capri
with a load of drunken chorus girls

in Hollywood the spot-lights went on in front of all
the gas stations and all
the laundromats
and seven thousand starlets stripped to the waist
and sang the Hallelujah chorus
riding camel-back up the Sunset Strip

up in mid-sky old Bodhidharma sat smiling gently
and scratching at his crotch
waiting for the man to ask the question
      so he could shrug his shoulders
            and split

Baby listen, I am the missionary of love
preacher of the gospel of the holy fuck, the great fuck, the good fuck
Sweetest of all finding your way through the flesh
burying your head in love, filling your mouth with love,
filling your hands with love, screaming your head off with love,
biting your teeth in love, caressing your tongue with love
Baby, what do you want
but the good fuck
really

Wonder Wander

in the afternoon the children walk like ducks
like geese
like from here to there
eyeing bird-trees puppy dogs candy windows
sun balls ice cream wagons
lady bugs rose bushes fenced yards vacant lots
tall buildings
and other things
big business men take big business walks
wear big business clothes
carry big business briefcases talk about
big business affairs in
big business voices
young girls walk pretty on the streets
stroll the avenues linger by
shop windows wedding rings lady hats
shiny dresses fancy shoes
whisper like turkey hens passing the time
young men stride on parade dream headed
wild eyed eating up the world
with deep glances rubbing empty fingers
in their pockets and
planning
me, I wander around soft-shoed easy-legged
watching the scene as it goes
finding things sea-gull feathers pink baby roses
every time I see a letter on the sidewalk
I stop and look it might be
for me
gladly alive me, I meander around smile-footed
big-eyed hands in my pockets
in my pretty afternoon

Poem for Ann

unloved ladies and dawn girls
    weeping your yellow hair at empty
                windows I will sing
      a song for you the
    sound of footsteps
remembering under your heel soft ladies
          pale violets crushed by early spring
    even as you with your painful mouth
and morning at your eyelids
            poured your wild hair over last night's
    dying blooms
I will sing for you ladies
the sound of footsteps . . .

Rocking in the rain
and springtime sprouting up
between my toes
I wove my hair with ashcan flowers
and sprinkled incense on the evening air
Brothers, I said, the millennium is here!
Forget
the lost art of basket weaving
Abandon your straitjackets
Come up from underground and
take a breath of
this
and up and down the street
there was a great awakening
Windows slid open and people leaped
holding umbrellas as parachutes
and blooming like flowers in the purple air
Naked, we danced ring-around-a-rosy
till after midnight
when the heavens parted
and a chorus of silver nightingales
walked out singing
So be it
in three-part harmony

Steazoned in heazell, by candlelight,
Hearing the wings bat against the icy breath of time
I shared the mourners' bench with a two-headed head
Listening to the pouty testimony of a would-be convert.
Listen baby, I wanted to say, go home
Pull your fuzzy eyelids down over your toes and
go back to sleep
Hell is for angels.
Only the mighty are fallen
Only the sun-touched can plummet
to these depths.
Go home, sinner, go home and sin some more
Stay up all night giggling at your own daring
Later, in good time, you can repent
and climb the gilded escalator
But remember
Hell is for angels.

Rebirth

Whom shall I with tender touch destroy
and then what nicety of fate
waits for my quiet step
as like a mindless mouse I walk the lotus wheel
wearing desire as a phoenix chain
this time again

Changeling

Penny baby walked the street
casting for sparrows with a hollow hand
hair (the color of morning) to her elbows
and whispering feet
tigers peered from windows, angels swam tree tops
green grass sang love songs
when she reached the end of the world
she was a sun flower
six foot tall
                    and toward heaven
sparrows ate her heart out as summer ended
and yellow turned to brown

Scarey Song

Mad children with grimy scissor fingered hands
cut faceless paper dolls
in hideouts underneath the sea
tunneling the coral wilderness
and whispering
in old silk voices
Their skins are blue and green and sliding
and they have borrowed dolphin's eyes
all day long, all night
their voices rustle
cutting paper dolls from clam shells
and moonbeams
under the turning tide
Mad children with flat and staring eyes
hide in the walls
thinner than shadows
catching our words in
thin brown knapsacks
and pelting them at the wind
Mad children with huge and heavy heads
sit one room away
whispering
I know . . . I don't know . . .
I know . . . I don't know . . .
All day long

Watching the Veiled Moon

Watching the veiled moon
I am a sea-gull in a grey-green world
Winging my way beyond the edge of night
Listen!   Listen to my heart beat!
The waves are my pulse
My wings are cloud-cutters.
I fly beyond the edge of night
And am gone.

Witch Song

Who am I? Who am I!
I am the witch of the mountains
daughter of the oak and the aspen
the brook and the stone
my mother turned into the moon
and birthed me in a flow of stars
I have no hands nor lips
and I am dying of love
Listen!   I am tapping at the window
tapping at the door
but the wind picks me up under his arm
and races me off to China
Listen!   I am the witch of the mountains
and I am dying of love

Grey-Beast

There is a loneliness upon my heart
that sits with grey wings folded
Lidless eyed and staring
It has no mouth to speak, my loneliness
no ears to hear
But crouches silent
nibbling the edges of my life

Woods Poem

I think I'll build an unhouse
somewhere near sweet water, near a stream
with a green garden
                                        anywhere
and thirteen nodding trees

the nicest thing about an unhouse
is that it's already.

Someday When We Are Strangers

someday when we are strangers . . .
    I will have forgotten you . . .
    I will have forgotten you . . .
and we will pass each other by along some April street and
        never know

east was the color of my love's dead eyes was
east was morning was last year sad was
death was dead his eyes were maggots oh
I have forgotten my love I have forgotten
my name I have
applied for a job in a dime store I have
dyed my hair topaz honey and learned to play at smiles
accepted the bodies of strangers and
become one

there is no end to dying it
happens all day long

I have never seen a nightingale.
I have, however, on summer days stopped in fascination
at the convolutions of a drying dog turd
I have also noted small patches of green moss at the edge of sewers
and on city sidewalks
in broken places
These alone would be more than enough
without midnight birds
but I have bought one rose for a penny on a sweaty New York street
and had a waitress buy me a whiskey sour on my birthday
and once I was invited to a party
by the nine year hostess
and danced musical chairs while
the adults sat mumbling in the adjoining room

Don't talk to me about nightingales.

City Night

The night stands waiting by my window
till lights grow on the hills like signal fires
and the fog curls its loving arms around night
and the city
kissing all the secret places
over and over again.

Ah love, I had not meant to leave
But when I woke, the wind had changed
And so had I.

In the Bitter Hours of Night

In the bitter hours of the night, sharing my room
with cockroaches that hang the walls like jewels
I remember Mexico
    remember Mazatlan, the colors of blue
                                    and gold and green
that were the world
the islands, the pale ocean, and the great light of day
illuminating our nakedness to the brilliance of Eden
    Later, the church where Christ was a
                              yellow-headed baby doll
clutching a money box
    . . . down payment on heaven . . .
At night we lay on the sea wall
    licking the saltspray from our tender lips

Hero the Rider

hero the rider sinless
windblasted through moonlight nights

man-engine
VULCAN THE CRIPPLED GOD conceived you with his metallic
sperm
raping the juicy thighs of Venus most maculate
beneath the volcano

!Hero!
screaming night agony over tract circle purgatories
racing the two wheel penis through world-universe intersections

hero the sinless rider

HERO THE WINDSUCKER

HERO THE HALFGOD
HERO THE nevermore wrapped in ashes buried in junkyards

torn by lions untouched . . .

HERO THE PERIPHERAL ANGEL INVENTOR OF THE WHEEL
AND INNOCENCE

hero the black leather saint of the virgins

ora pro nobis

now and at the hour of your death

The Time of the Golden Bull

In the shadow of the moon
the townsmen gelded the golden bull
that had walked the hills and the vallies
and shook the fruit from the trees
with his voice
The women at night in their beds
had shivered their delicate flesh
at his call
trembled their soft white breasts
the girl children stirred in their sleep
sighing and dreaming
dreaming with their hands between their legs
and their skin flushed and shining
The townsmen grew angry, heard his brass-bright voice
as a challenge
and grew angry
Met in the taverns and the walled houses, saying
we must make him harmless, he's a threat to our women
dropping their hands and guarding their sex
they said, he is dangerous, frightening, destructive
it is our duty
we must capture and hold him
nodding their heads they went home to their beds
The metal voice of the bull boomed through the night
and they dreamed their plans into snares, into ropes,
into knives.

The golden bull walked with delicate feet
on the yielding ground
His right forefoot brushed the daisies
and he lowered his head to green young grass
snuffing the wet air
from the earth dark roots
The moon burst the clouds like a bridal veil
hanging his pointed horns with silver

tinsel horns, diamond horns, jabbing the tender air
as he pawed the earth
with his dancing feet
crushing the juice of small flowers
with his quick hooves, raising his heavy head
and bellowing
challenge to the maiden moon
snorting his wild nostrils, his bellow
smashed the night like a hammer on glass
rousing the townsmen from their sleeping cocoons
stirring the blood of the delicate women
till they reached for their husbands
with trembling thighs

The bull roared, rocking the night like a wave
snipping the thread between the hours with his plunging hooves
as he ran
pounding the night into chaos, over
the hills, beside the brook, beside the trees
bending the branches as he stamped and screamed challenge
to the wide black night

In the morning the townsmen gathered
their eyes glistening
in the silky light of dawn
They built an enclosure, a trap, swinging their hammers
through the morning
heavy hammers through the sunlight of the day
and baited it with a young white cow
tethered her there
leaving her to low the ache of her heat
into the winds of noon
They climbed the trees then, the townsmen
they hung in the branches
like sullen fruit

waiting for the bull to answer
the wailing of the anguished cow
They heard him come running, wild hooves
racing him closer
racing the meadow the river the hills
heard his voice swallow the whole of the morning
shout it out in a tempest

He stood there, the bull, stamping and steaming
his golden hide gleaming the rays of the noon sun
echo of heaven, burnished pale armor
he raced for the heifer, his wild mouth screaming
Quietly, fruit from the branches, they dropped
ran soft through the grasses, scurrying man mice
swung the vast gate shut and locked it with iron
brushed their wet hands on their sides
and stood back
hearts trembling they watched the bull
mount the plunging white heifer
their bellies tightened, grew hard with his need
oh how the bull roared, the heifer was lowing
the townsmen were sweating with fear at their catch

Releasing the heifer the bull stood there panting
shaking his strong, his terrible head
the heifer was silent, the townsmen stood frozen
the bull raised his head, sniffed the white afternoon
heels flying he raced for the meadow, the woodland
slammed his broad horns at the thick wooden fence
then for the first time he knew he was captured
then for the first time he bellowed his rage
shrieking he battered the walls with his body
turning and charging each side of the trap
the wooden walls shivered but stood unrelenting
The men heaved a sigh and unclenched their tight fists

watching the wild bull charge in his terror
the men stood there watching, their hands at their sides
We'll let him grow tired, they said starting homeward
back to the town, to their suppers and wives
let him expend all his strength on the wood walls
racing in circles and crying his rage
let him grow weary with charging the fences
later, at evening, we'll come back again
in the cool of the evening we'll come back again

In the shadow of night with the sad moon rising
crying her long white tears
they walked up the road in the moonlight
swinging their well-fed arms
the bull stood like rock in the moonlight
waiting till they came near
his muscles quivered with anger
as he pawed the turned up ground
and he bellowed thunder and lightening
and charged with horns held low
he failed once more and he stood there
dark stone in the quiet of night
stood like a rock in the shadows
under the pale moon's tears
They roped and they tied and they bound him
they laughed like schoolboys in springtime
and boasted their pride to each other
side-watching the shuddering bull
the bravest of all (so they named him)
wielded the flickering knife
silver and gold in the moonlight, swallowed
by red, by the blood

Black scarlet flowed in the moonlight
when they gelded the golden bull

he screamed with the terror of ages
and knelt
under the weight of his rage
His blood melted the earth like a river
while they watched with bitter dark eyes
and he screamed like Gabriel's trumpet
and rolled on his side and died

But why did he die, said the townsmen
drifting their pale way home
why did he die, said the townsmen
brushing their hands on their thighs
and the virgin moon hung crying
over the silent world

Afternoon of a Phoenix

I sit as sweet and sullen as a child
holding the string of my balloon and
watching passersby
through eyelashes turned into screens
I sit upon the granite wall that
rims the park—moss island on the city rock—
and when the sun grows dim
I loose the string—my
blue balloon sails high
and I—I stand up straight and tall
and grow as old as you—nor wiser than—
and wish my blue balloon were mine again

Phoenix Song

then I shall never grow up
not if child means a sense of wonder
and my head in the wind rain sun
I will not wither in the blaze of time
but prove myself a phoenix
                    (ashes like powdered stars)
born again   and again   and again

girl story

Her breasts grew like wild flowers
in the rainy spring, in the summer
she and the strawberries turned sweet and ripe
and toward the sun

Fog-Bound

only sea gulls ride the fog
cutting the clouds with wild wings
and making moan
over dying waves.

Old Lady Poem

skull-headed old ladies
ornamenting their decay with imitation pearls
they walk beside me along sidewalks
tombstones of black earth and unborn trees
we ride together endless omnibuses
and I find them beside me at the Goodwill
scuffling for old silk underwear and broken enemas
they crowd the markets
buying one lambchop and a jar of beets
and I have seen them stealing newspapers
from my front steps
stuffing them into their huge black bags

sometimes they smile at me

No Clock No Time

oh yes I am beautiful and yes you are beautiful lying here with my blue-
jeaned buttocks against the grey rug there are leaves on the floor where
the wind left them dry my fingers break them like spices drift out again
like heavy dust I lie there listening to Anita O'Day in the after noon
laughing bubbles my body up and down but silent I smile sit up and
drink my beer the sun warms my warm shoulders filtering through
long tall glass called windows   ah sweet not insane but unsane asane
who questions the mind of god gives IQ tests to angels pins down the
sex life of rivers   today this morning started with pink geraniums
and peeing among the fallen leaves I watched the stream of my urine
dark the ground flow downhill makes islands in the dust concentrating
miraculous flow out of me changing the earth wet where it was dry
watch it pour out of me hot from my insides steaming squeeze my
muscles pushing off the last small drops and empty bladdered walking
back feeling the early of it all   no clock no time
this now house lives way up and take a lot of walking to   I stand spread
legged and watch the trees dance while my breath cools down feet on
red brick beside the welcome door of old house   and now against the
nubby carpet's grey dirt feel good to my fingers   look can I explain
to you the sharing we made three of us and love I keep forgetting
you know everything   god is omniscient and can spell all the words
I am woman times twelve I am mathematics purified by jazz I am a
lump of love surrounded by words and we have dined today on pretty
dexamyls lifting little pills with dainty fingertips into the cavern of my
mouth flooding beer down my intestinal yardage rainbow slack and
wind-y   my toes are like fingers long and shaped sensitive I could
caress you with my feet there is no part of my body ignorant of love
today I combed my hair with my fingers   long hair long fingers had
no needed no comb washed my face in cold water and let the morning
dry it wiping my hands along my sides   happy   and YES and YES
and I won't STOP I'm going to cross America by pogo stick curious I
smell my skin bending my head to my forearm enjoying the smell of
myself the skin warm from the sun releasing its spicy oils shadow of

blue veins examining the small lines of my hands raise my eyes to the
green glass window and vision of beyond   Monk is talking to himself
out loud and we are rolling careful cigarettes in wheat straw paper why
you smoke them skinny cigarettes, mama?   sucking sweet smoke
and autumn air the ritual tight mouth pass to the finger burning lip
singeing end my tweezer nails are scorched ten days of friendly turn
on this one too much   the beer cans are breeding covering the floor I
lie back wishing I could turn somersaults listen to the flood of bright
beautiful words counterpointing old Monk through the high vault room
us angels soar   purity purity untrackable purity outside the trees are
whispering making poetry about us sending broken leaves through the
door every time the wind blows it blows often rolling another joint I
watch those tender fingers
good words we blow good words better silences
another heart shaped bitter pill we brush fingers in gnomic ritual
sipping slow beer   blending sweet roach ends in the tip of a cigarette
you pass it to me hanging billiard eyed to the door post I suck in deeply
and turn to stone barely able to pass it on transfixed too beautiful at
the edge of fear one step beyond control bees in my veins terror awed
crouched there aware of room grey rug green window books records
music spiraling down can't do a thing butterfly pinned to a postcard
heavy armed too far out COME BACK
can't breathe and then I can and high but here again frightened let
my breath out but already regretting my return too much to take but
worth it look around as one returned from the dead   time travel   east
yesterday sip beer like salvation holding the pure reality beer can peer
the room around catching the spark of your eye and break up laughing
WITH YOU so with so part of fat warm feeling floods through me
I stay quiet and appreciate feel it flow through my body elbows and
fingernails across the room the green window is built of little panes of
glass irregular glass if I ran my fingers over it it would be like tracing
a relief map it would be a relief but getting up I stare out the kitchen
window face to face with frongy trees a bird flies by gasping me at his

calm these trees are eucalyptus trees their bark hangs like witches hair
the wind is blowing eucalyptus nuts against the window I am leaning
on sunlight sitting between you I form a triangle you whisper to me
squatting by my side that this is how they shit in China you shout to me
with your phosphorescent eyes
how beautiful we are   and we are   and we are

Poem for a Long-Gone Lover

Lonely is a razor blade
and I could bleed to death waiting for you

without you night is emptybed and endless
    the bed is too big
    the night is too cold

Love hurts   you never told me that
when you kissed me

Grant Avenue

they say there's this city ordinance against wandering
I'm guilty
ignorance of the law is no excuse but I've seen
NO PARKING signs
NO SPITTING signs NO SMOKING signs lots
of other NO signs
but I've never seen a NO WANDERING sign
yet

thank god

the dictionary says wandering is: roaming at will,
traveling
I say it's also a way of life
open to the world like a sea anemone to a rich green wave
I absorb the flowers the faces and the words
I devour the multitude
I swallow the universe
and all and everything of it becomes myself
the wonder of the world is my most essential food
and my absolute and alchemical body
would starve without it
I am a sea creature, a star creature, a human creature
no man can legislate my being

I reveal my belly to delight
    expose my toes and navel
        deliver up my joints and apertures
even as earth to rain in its season
what was dry becomes moist   becomes damp
    I explode under you
    like an enormous jungle flower
    bursting
in the wet heat of planetary love

afraid to sleep alone
we tangle in my narrow bed
pressing loveless to loveless
    — small comfort
but some

Small Hours Poem

I dream of death as sparrows dream of hawks
a presence up above and just beyond the eye
    a darkness in the sky

old bone man sits within my own sweet flesh
waiting me out with cool white patience

there are times he entices me
in the narrow part of night, when I begin to lose faith in morning
and I am all and entirely alone

yet somehow night always ends in time and he lets go
he has the patience of an owner
as he slips inside
and loans me back my own white bones again
this contract is one-sided, old man!

he winks and sits inside
I shrug my borrowed bones and laugh at both of us

the morning smells so sweet . . .

Storm July

sweetly birds swim past my window
frozen by my eye against the sky of wind
birdflight   windform   treeburst
my room is warm
and soon the rain begins

sweet love I have lost my words lost my praises
kissing your mouth
lost my words in the warm in the hunger
of your mouth
in the deep silk of your skin sweet love
lost my words
only you and I love our hands small animals
caress
our bodies meet bursting like stars
you and I love
peering through my lashes you are too beautiful to bear
I am drowning in this honey ocean only know kisses
only know whispers
I have lost my words and answers only you and I love
bursting like stars

Epilogue

And you will comfort me when I am dead
and angels comb my hair with feathered wings
when I am drifting down the wind as light
as far off voices in a far off fog
will your hands catch me
your fingers seine me like a precious fish
and will you breathe me back to life
when I am dead love when I am dead
and have kissed angels with my bloodless mouth

my love the fisherman comes back smelling of salt dying
his ocean arms embrace me and
I taste the death of seals on his thin mouth

they eat the fish—and so
he shoots them with a .22
sighting among the green waves

so do we, I think
wondering if the seals
will ever invent gunpowder

Museum Concert

I couldn't help noticing the lady   elegant beside
her thirteen year old lover of an alien race
he moved his hand   /the fingers of a conscious man/
against her back
assurance in the subtle stroke
his head   /seraph face or newborn succubus/
nuzzled to her thick bosom

the orchestra played Bach

Fuck/Angel

angel, fuck/angel, beautiful/angel, beautiful, beautiful,
beautiful
yours are the wings, the gold and scarlet plumaged wings,
the flame-tipped blood-red wings
that fan the love-sick bodies of incandescent lovers
into a radiance unendurable beautiful beautiful
angel, love/angel, fuck/angel, glory, glory
I have felt the flame edge of your feathers
against my most tender parts
and I have FELT the Flame and glory,
glory, angel, fuck/angel, you are no minion of emasculated gods
you were there at Olympian orgies of uncalculated celestial lust
you attended the thousand Krishnas delighting the herd-girls
causing the wind to blow sweet and the grass to grow tender
you are a manifestation of love and your body is radiance
I hear the sigh of your incredible wings
as we lie transfixed with love
love/angel fuck/angel beautiful
beautiful beautiful beautiful

Poem for Sunday Riders

artichokes they grow like wild birds, batting their green feathers
in the roadside wind
we pass by the universe observers in a rusty chevy
as the ocean turns circus and five hundred sea lions leap like
rainbows
arcing in triplicate from wave to wave
leading us to laugh in pure delight to stop at pigeon point
applauding in gratitude
laughter turning to almost tears   wonder at pure beauty
big sleek dark forms spinning across the wild sea
we lean against a barbed wire fence
(visitors prohibited on lighthouse grounds)
too struck to envy
still laughing at the next town
and all the afternoon way back

now entering this market in sandaled feet and brow pulled big
black hat
I peer over the carrots port wine one reddest apple for my lovely lunch
and we drive on drive sucking the sweet bottle and over
dirt and backwoods roads
reaching ultimately the same place we started from
all filled with
sunday satisfaction
and off to other scenes remembering
above all
the pure wonder of sea lions
breaking black rainbows on the green gray waves

If all day long you had had a perfectly beautiful Tuesday
                    and the next morning
you bought a newspaper and it said "Thursday"
would that make the day before any less Tuesday?

*

If a friend cooked you some really delicious mushroom soup
and you said to him, "This is great mushroom soup"
      and he said
Thank you, but it's potato
would that make it any less mushroom?

Rose Dream

ladies dream of roses
        pink ladies   red roses
ladies dream of roses in their ornate drawing rooms
wearing rich and rare perfumes
at their wrists and at their earlobes
dream of red and crimson roses   velvet roses in profusion
blooming rich and thick and potent
                through the shadows of the room
        hollow rooms where ladies dream
teardrops gleam like crystal
                as they fall among the roses
        where love has gone away
ladies dream of roses in their empty drawing rooms
wearing rich and rare perfumes
scented   like Egyptian mummies
in their secret silent tombs

Vernal Equinox Forecast—1968

the star ram wakes in the green heavens
his head is garlanded with flowers
and he sets his feet on the path of fire
the children walk beside him
offering themselves to each other
they walk through the fire and survive
the inn-keeper fears the flame
and tries to flee
but he has waited too long
the building is become a desert
and the landlord is a stranger to himself

the star ram walks the planet
and his hooves strike fire from the earth
all the seeds that have been planted
bloom
the flowering weed destroys the vaults of marble
the onlooker finds no shelter from the wind
the children build houses together
sharing their tools and their love songs
offering themselves to each other
they walk through the fire
and survive

new consciousness arises

old men
practice misdirection on the young men
young men
genuflect to bomb-god
and get in line to die
dead men
they cannot make a child

old men
your youth was yesterday
how dare you from the safety of your years
reach out to cancel the tomorrows
of one living human fool

young men
alliance with murder is murder
that murderer is victim of his crime

dead men
what good are you to those
who would have loved you
as you died, did you whisper
'this is it, what I wanted'
as your death fell across the death
of women and children
and brothers of your covenant with life

Christians, you who call yourself
Christians
does your machine-gun Jesus bless the napalm
as it eats the living bones of children
is the shrill of their agony   as birdsong
to his angel ears
Christians, you who call yourself
Christians
are the bombs you drop sanctified
are your bullets holy

does your Christ of Destruction walk beside you
saying
'kill, for death is my benediction
saying
'blessed are the warmakers, for they shall
destroy it all
saying
'let the children come unto me
but let them come blind and crippled and maimed
let them come crawling on their screaming bellies
with the flesh of their bodies melting into flame
and the agony of their dying shall be my kingdom
saying
'this is your brother; destroy him,
that his death may remain with you
throughout the days of your life

destroy him
so that sight of his death
be indelible upon your eyes
that the sound of his death
be indelible upon your ears
that the fact of his death
be indelible upon your hands
that his death may remain with you
throughout the nights of your life
Christians, you who call yourself
Christians
what have you done with your Christ
that his church is a napalmed baby
that his cross is hung with a rifle
that 'Amen' is said with a bomb

old men
young men

dead men
mothers and lovers and strangers
what does it mean
that you say peace
and spread death
that you say love
and spread death
that you say freedom
and spread death

what does it mean that you're silent
when silence
is assent to murder

what does it mean duty
when young men come home
dead meat in wood boxes

Americans, you who call yourself
Americans
let not that name become a curse
on the tongue of a dying world
Americans, you who call yourself
Americans
consider what you pledge allegiance to
allegiance to bomb-god
is death of a planet
allegiance to napalm
is invocation of hell
Americans, you who call yourself
Americans
if you become afraid to speak your conscience
it is all the more urgent that you speak
and speak loudly

there is no middle ground
old man
there is no middle ground
young man
there is no middle ground
dead man

there is no middle ground

Hawaiian Mountain

Up here on the mountain there is nothing to forget
whatever is is incontestable
The sun rising over the eastern trees
starts the earliest birds
spiraling their songs against the sky
and the luminous light of dawn exposes the land
the coarse thick grass of the pastures glows with a living green
lush, vibrant, a brilliance that accosts the eye
the trees are various,
groves of a darker green edging the hilly ridge
silver leaved solitaries, and dead bare branches
mock foliated with pale green and vivid orange lichens
not many flowers grow this high
small crimson secrets that bloom hidden in the grass
a million insects scuttle through the larder of the day
the spider hanging watchful in his web
Full moon and the sun illuminates my mind
I sit on the edge of the cliff, trying to discern the difference
between my body and my thought
watching the white waves of the ocean stand frozen
twenty six hundred feet below my toes
brown-and-white and black the cattle dot the pastures
eating their way through bovine eternity
chewing oblivion with their grass-pale white lashed eyes
The clouds blow white across the sky
descending now and then to hang in the tree tops
or drift across the valleys below the mountain
and I look down on clouds
At evening the sun rolls below the ocean horizon
banners of light across the sky-glass of the Pacific
black lava coast, and the waters roll out
toward the sunset horizon
At night I listen to the stars, articulate prisms of the night
the resonance of light is music
and the air vibrates with rainbow flickers

connecting star and star across the plains of space
the moon hangs liquid in the sky, mad mirror of my dreams
sweet silver light chime-tinkling in my brain
later the wind blows, playing the planetary harp
arpeggios that echo in my breath

Up here on the mountain there are no façades to the universe
defenses of the civic mind negate themselves
and the search for the spirit totem claims the star
not earth alone has built this mountain nor this me
but earth one facet of the universal jewel
this light that pulses through the sky is part of me and I of it
this mountain and myself, life-rooted in oceanic earth
I stand upon its slopes of dormant fire
learning to listen
one more expansion of the unexpectant eye

Hymn to Maitreya in America

3000 miles across the continent, ocean to ocean
crossing the paths of cities like
barnacles across the fat back of the land
grass lands, wheat lands, sage deserts
where gold bones lie buried beneath hallucinatory cacti

Maitreya who is the only buddha who sits in Western posture
Maitreya the buddha of love who is the fifth and final buddha
of our cycle
Maitreya who is growing from the ground of America in
polymorphous immediacy
the necessity of survival demanding his presence
five hundred years before his time

obeisance to all gurus

obeisance to all gurus

obeisance to all gurus

obeisance to all gurus

I see Maitreya in the miracle of leaf and bud, in the flower
that ignites from the plant
a rooted butterfly

I see Maitreya in the rock of the bones of the mountain
in the speaking-silence of its sempiternal wisdom ashana

I see Maitreya in the unchanging-change of the motion body of the
river

man-child I see Maitreya in the fact of your existence and in the
existence of that which is beneath your feet and that which is on
the other side of your eye

I see Maitreya in the vision of the existence of Maitreya and in
the vision of the existence of myself and in the vision of existence and
in the vision of beyond existence

obeisance to all gurus

consider that within the center of the wind there sits a dakini-angel
her robes are the blue of newborn eyes and she wears a necklace of
raindrops
she is never silent but her voice is as soft as a selfless tear
for a thousand times a thousand years she has sung the song of
The Gem Cloud of Arising Consciousness
she will never be silent until the wind is still

consider that within the center of the earth there sits a dakini-angel
her robes are the red of a man's blood and she wears a necklace of
human finger bones
she is never silent but her voice is the echo of silence
for a thousand times a thousand years she has sung the song of
The Heart Knowledge of Undivided Awareness
she will never be silent until the earth is still

consider that within the center of the oceans there sits a dakini-angel
her robes are the green of winter moss and she wears a necklace of
pearl shells
she is never silent but her voice is as quiet as snow that falls on water
for a thousand times a thousand years she has sung the song of
The Self Mirror of Perfect Light
she will never be silent until the sea is still

consider that within the center of the sunbeam there sits a dakini-angel
her robes are the orange-yellow of pollen and she wears a necklace of
burning flowers
she is never silent but her voice is as soft as the dust of dust
for a thousand times a thousand years she has sung the song of

The Rainbow of the Wakening Dream
she will never be silent until the sun is still

I see Maitreya in America
the smoke of machinery rises to his left hand
and the smoke of incense rises to his right hand
he joins his hands and the bird of existence
flies from between his fingers
flashing its seven-colored wings across the continent
and circling back to whisper at his feet

he stand within the center of reality
and his left hand and his right hand weave a net
of the perimeters of the mind
and the net is infinite
and the infinite net is cast into itself

and I see Maitreya in America
he stands within the center of reality
and his left hand and his right hand are raised
his left hand is in the gesture of compassion
and his right hand is in the gesture of awakening

and I see Maitreya in America
Maitreya the fifth and final buddha of our cycle
Maitreya the buddha of love
and he stands within the center of infinity
and between his left hand and his right hand
he holds the clear light mirror

and the mirror reflects

Muir Beach Mythology/September

Horses that run beside the sea
heads proud as intergalactic swans
five horses, five riders
five sisters of Virgo   the vision of
September myth revealed
five blond-haired maidens perfect
in their bareback reality
manes of the autumnal centaur, the
banners of the equinox
This is the myth, the myth of September
it is a green meadow by the side of
a sea beach by the side of the Pacific horizon
the five girls ride down from the mountains
lady centaurs at afternoon play
three of them hold white kittens in their bosoms
and their long hair flows over the wind
plumes of splendor across the cusp of Libra's angel
behind them a young colt comes dancing
weaving the white nets of winter
Expectations of incredible spring

Excerpt from a Prayer Wheel

I offer you one hundred ways of love
dreams of enlightenment and shadow plays of joy

consider yourself new-born: open your eyes and note the swirling
    of infinite reality
extend your hand to another being: experience the texture of skin
    against your finger-tips; be aware of the crevices of your hand
    and how another's flesh can fill them
assume you are a star: allow the atoms of your psyche to expand and
    become planets circling your star; observe the orbits into which
    they fall
become a bee exploring the orange-yellow tunnel of a nasturtium: feel
    the pollen accumulating on your velvet legs; faint from the smell
    of heaven
become a giant phallus, swollen with blood and rigid with self-righteousness;
    open your single eye and demonstrate the spew of life
become an enormous cunt, pulsating at the moment of orgasm: learn what
    tides and earthquakes are all about
become one snowflake in a total blizzard: fall all the way to earth;
    melt, and feed yourself to whatever needs you
become an oceanic shellfish: float free in the sea as a baby and then
    attach yourself to a rock with tiny tendrils and open your calcified mouth
    to the passing tide
be a candle: feel the flame ignite you, burn brightly giving your
    entire body to the flame; a candle has nothing to hold back
become an angel: observe yourself in a large mirror; note any
    similarities to your previous state
become a vortex at the edge of infinity: devour the winds of space
    and sing the song of your own true being

become a diamond sparkling on the hand of a politician's call-girl
become a diamond thirty miles beneath the surface of the earth enjoying

    your own interior radiance in the middle of darkness
become a mythical bird that eats diamond as gravel to help digest worms

become your own imagination: float back and look at your own head
    move in any direction you wish
there is nothing but truth; there is nothing but illumination
assume you are the next buddha; act toward me in this way

Dead Billy

you're a long way gone from here, Billy
body becoming earth and the rest of you farther than star light
messages across the green glaciers of interstellar drift
death alters the reference points
when I think of you I look beyond Orion
maybe I see a tarot deck spinning through a magician's hands
or your smile rising in the Bat nebula
somewhere beyond the bend of space
the tenderest memory I have of you is you completely nodded out
clasping your baby in the total security of unfeigned love
you were a green flame of unacceptable truth
and you ring like a zen bell
spiraling through infinity like you always knew the way home

dry man

there is something perfect in your agony
the lucid tension with which you dissect your hesitant certainties
the drunken disasters that propel you screaming through the night
lean naked body howling against the walls of what purports to be home
outpost of order in the decimation of love
perfect, the tremor of your hand avoiding destruction by one more
cataclysmic leap into chaos
the thin order of clarity sorting your mind without mercy
and your conscience without ease
leaving not even the privacy of your balls
to rest mindless
but each cell and sinew of your flesh laid out by starlight
to live or die by its own intrinsic weight
one gram of flesh, one glimpse of love
the prometheus flame
cupped in the chalice of your burning spine

prayer on the wind

when the wind blows hard enough
there is nothing left but stars
everything else, all the accoutrements of safety
all the placebos of habit
are blown away
even the stars tremble slightly
to a fine-edged eye

you have no pity, lord
only compassion

the road is long and long enough
hard and hard enough
over the bones of love and the ashes of dreams

you have no pity, lord
only compassion

pity offers no end to pain
the passing comfort
of a tear in the desert
compassion burns like a knife
dissecting the root of agony in clear daylight

there must be an end to suffering
let me cause no more pain
let me spread no more pain
let the pain that comes to me
end with me

let me have no pity, lord
only compassion

seven of velvet

brocade and tapestry, you lean back, your head against the blue velvet
and the sun dancing sparks of light across your naked skin
you lie there, your balls nibbled by teen-aged succubi
and your hands on their snaky heads
their moonglow fingers twining around your rigid cock
and their little tongues darting and licking
as you stroke their smoky hair

across the room, I lie between the paws of a tiger
almost faint from the scent of his violent fur
he holds me to his belly and his paws bind me
his huge head purring like thunder at my shoulder
his white belly is velvet against me
and I am velvet to him

slowly, subtly, his paws tighten around me
and he enters within my body
I look at you from the embrace of the tiger
and our eyes meet in wonder
little tongues, little hands, move faster
and you cry out as you come
spurting a fountain of flowers
into the tiger's mouth

Quantum Choreography

reality moves like a dancer
spaceless and graceless, mutably more perfect than time
I have always known the language, I was born of it,
            the cellular murmur
the form of reason a grid to shape amorphous mind
a crystalline lattice for my psyche to chime against
narcissus eggs of self-refractive light
cosmos spoken here, I am a dancer
a permeable envelope of motion
fishing the night for concepts almost remembered
my self and a star, we are of the same order of being
as a star spins planets
the heat of my consciousness
maintains this whirl of matter that I call my flesh
no sun exists but I am kin to it
am I a galaxy to sentients musing in my blood, my breath?
who charts the constellations of my mind?
I think about I like a series of trick mirrors
hoping to catch myself unaware
and it never stops moving
I am a dancer
      and I dance
            I dance
                  I dance

Everyday Magic

Were I a wise woman in the hill tribes
rough jewels hung in my grease slick hair
and dreams spewing out of my mouth
as I chanted by the dawn fire
raising my arms with the flight of the wild birds
sky trumpet knife wing
that lifts the light
the daywind is blowing out the stars
scatter, spirits that walk between the worlds!
rejoin your yesterdays once more
run, night children!
run to your holes and dens
creep to the roots of grandfather oak

thus and thus I would sing, I would chant
I would squat in the thin cold dust and stare to the fire
gleaning revelation from ember and flame and the tracing of sparks

I would have a skin bag with a certain feather
fever come here and fever go
I would have a skin bag filled with everyday magic
rare stones and bones and herbs that grow
where the clouds hide the mountain

this I would do that the people grow stronger
that the young grow wise and the wise be loving
that the earth bear us lightly
that the night give us shelter
that the day give us laughter
that we share with each other
with the eagle with the salmon
with the bear with the otter
with the planet with the stars
may it be

the pot bird story

waking half waking mouth open eyes shut and legs grabbing at
each other with breath subsiding as the juices dry our eyelids flicker
up we reach beside the bed for the artful joint so wisely placed the
night before and sip with tender mouths (still cradled in each other's
flesh) when suddenly at once eyes gently peering to the window left
we see the flash of yellow birds swarm the trees like locusts hopping
claw footed over green leaf waysides soft bird-shaped birds as never
seen before their egg and butter winging bodies and silver heads and
pure surprise
what are they? half wondering if you see them too and small relief as
you whisper in my ear, pot birds, you say I don't believe you, I answer
sure of your truth as I deny it, what color are they? yellow you tell me
and what can I say to that so yellow they are yellower than anything
I've ever known and so you see them too and both of us so sweetly
high and are you right after all, pot birds? and we sit there warm in bed
and watching
they only show up when you're high one right there! two over there!
and twenty and ten and yellow each more bird than bird has ever been
and dance the tree into yellow bird heaven until suddenly all gone and
we arise at noon washing our faces with soft water from a leaky tap
each morning waking then with one eye turned toward birds and never
finding only empty green and tarnished trees and waking then with
love and coffee but neither pot nor birds nor quite convinced of their
alliance but wondering and morning sitting over breakfast smoking
thin cigarettes for lunch gave quick look at window and they were back
a revelation of angels swarming the trees with yellow feather wings the
pretty birds leaping limb to limb pot birds, you smiled I nodded and
sat there watching the abundance of yellow with the smoke drifting
through the interstices of my long long bones

Gregory . . . .

In New Mexico
He put his rumpled body
between me and the police
when the DA swore he'd arrest
me for reading my poetry

Here, when I was motorcycle smashed
he cooked dinners for me
that I couldn't eat

His heart was as tender as
a cactus without any spines
a rose with soft thorns

A Place to Stand

Air itself is light
sweet morning in a bridal veil
all possibility inherent
in each breath

I cast my mind out to the vast beyond
as it were a lariat
or else a fishing line
I troll for enlightenment, for epiphany
I troll for grace
for a warm touch
among the chiming stars

V.

Unpublished Works

Afterword

when love is ended there are no songs to play
no feast of yesterdays
only the small clear painful knowledge
that the windy candle has burned out
leaving only smoke
and the memory of a bright and perfect light

American Dreams

George Washington was never America's hero
no matter how many dollar bills they put his picture on
It was Jesse James, Billy the Kid, John Dillinger
set the legends flying
The outlaw is the archetype of glory
the secret hero of suburbia
nobody wants to fuck a cop
but the thighs of America's women grow steamy
as they dream of marauders
the paper pushers dream of violence as they fill out forms
the outlaw's dance with death
buggery and rape, drunken kaleidoscope of suck/fuck gangbang
haunting the secret dreams of the American tracts
THE HERO OF THE AMERICAN ID IS THE MOTORCYCLE OUTLAW
racing his screaming chopper
down the raw-nerved hypocritical spine of the country
(ten thousand faggots whirl in leather lust)
unwashed, uncombed, his genitals scummy with yesterday's perversities
the skeleton of his future invoked in present tense acceptance
riding invisibly obvious beside him NO FEAR OF DEATH!
(a million housewives creaming in their installment plan panties
yearning for luscious domination, the brutal male ramming his life size
penis CRAAACK through the opaque hymen of television boredom,
seven shadowy figures demanding indecent satisfactions, pauseless
obscenities, helpless,
ravaged, she's coming like a maniac, but it's all fantasy baby, married
twenty years nor ever sucked a cock and don't forget the young ones
rubbing their beautiful pussies against imagination's ultimate phallus,
god through gangbang, abandonment through I couldn't help it, he stuck
it up me when I wasn't looking, I came without consent)
fascination/obsession, hero of dirty daydreams, VIOLENCE goddamn
madman armed with guns knives chains tire irons brass
knuckles stomping boots KILL THE MOTHERFUCKER he'll do
anything smash your teeth fuck you in the ass rape your wife kill
you rob you gang stomp you violate you terrorize you

WHAT KIND OF ETHICS (oh the righteous indignation of the deodorized as they yearn to kill niggers, rob banks, cheat the system, smash the dissident, and dip their whining cocks into the dirty-cunted dirty-eyed dirty girls that they fantasize while crawling for the stale delights of nagging matrimony) and he sees his dreams made manifest, Mr. America of the mercantile empire, the hierarchy of ulcers, the tenacious yearning to explode anxiety into violence, the cringing nausea of repeated compromise, the longing for total commitment

the outlaw has released the fear of fear
inescapably alien, he walks with his death as a garland

there is no illusion of security
dancing a tightrope in the now of forever
the acrobat of disaster juggling his own eternity
gambling his skull against a case of beer
his bones against the wind
his blood against a definition of honor
THERE'S NOTHING TO LOSE
on the other side of fear
(oh and the mortgage, the life insurance, the pension, old age, taxes, atom bombs, the invisible mechanized rat gnawing the possibilities of man)
there is glamor in danger
teasing the reverie of a man unfulfilled with himself
there is magic in the burst tabu
DIR-ty
Dis-GUST-ing
Against the LAW
that twinges envy in those that fear their own dreams
the vision of the outlaw
using it all up
playing for keeps
OPEN ABUSE OF DECENCY AND HUMAN RIGHTS
enthralls and appalls the suburban inheritors of the American dream

descendants of
witch burners
slave breeders
Indian killers
treaty breakers
land stealers
sweatshop owners
whorehouse landlords
segregationist ministers
expedient politicians
overkill generals

sons and daughters of the Bill of Rights and the padded expense account,
blind-minded to the petty deceits of historic hypocrisy
waving a con-man's flag
it's your secret brain that shudders at itself
and claims the outlaw as hero
because he does it right out loud
because he wears his own shit like a halo
and lays his life on the line
without regret
if the bet is taken up
because regret
is a quality of doubt
and it's no longer a question of societal right and wrong
but his own definitions
backed by his existence
or his non-existence

and the outlaw is America's hero
secret companion of frightened fantasy thrills in the interchangeable
vacuums of dissatisfaction
because too many men have sold out their manhood
trading their visions for time payment lies
and too many women have bartered themselves for a facsimile of love

designed to impress the stranger
while their own hearts grow numb
and the outlaw is America's hero
because he is what he is
and neither begs pardon nor forgiveness nor mercy
and the nation is corroded by guilt

Angel

the eye sees what the mind expects
when the mind releases expectation
vision perceives
perception varies as the eye varies
as the mind varies
moving through Moebius infinity
until recognitions collide

Cherokee

it's kind of an Indian in-joke
almost every time an anglo comes up
and declares blood kin
and someone says what tribe
it turns out he's got a Cherokee or half-Cherokee grandma
never Kiowa or Comanche or Cree
and never a grandfather either
this friend of mine I hadn't seen in a couple years
showed up with feathers in her braids screaming about white eyes
I didn't know you were Indian I say
Oh yeah, didn't I ever tell you? my grandmother
What tribe I ask, sliding my glance over her left eyebrow
and hoping she'll say Modoc or Oglala Sioux or maybe Iroquois
Cherokee she says, and I nod
as I've nodded before
but maybe it's all true   or none of it is   or some of it is
but for sure those busy Cherokee ladies are chuckling away
in inscrutable eternity
'cause they loved riddles better than breakfast
and I can hear them giggling like swampbirds
at the unsortable joke they've left behind

CircumLocation

this is where *you* wanted to be, my friend
high on the mountain, eyes filled with planetary circumstance
wind blowing through your head
sunrise and sunset in the expanse of silence
me, I wasn't so eager
but here I am
while you, you're still in the city
running around the streets
sitting up all night in wild conversation
I haven't heard a telephone ring in three months
but I could swear I just heard a long distance laugh

Dancers Poem

Hey pretty thing, you so pretty when you dance!
You move in radiant grace
to sounds that make your breastbone ring

A Definition of Love

Love, that I watched you sleeping, that
I watched your face
calm on the white pillow
and felt no envy of your dreams
and switching off the light
slid naked beside you in our bed
still sleeping, you turned to me
and held me
which was the dream

Dope Poem

one of the things about dope is
you can never take a piss because
the bathroom is always full of people
shooting up
and you can't stir your coffee while you
wait
because all the spoons are gone
and when you find them hidden
behind the bathtub
you have to wash the soot off and
they don't taste right anyway
and if you take your turn and
sit on the john and
roll up your sleeve
it's only a hot flash
in a cold world

Excerpt

and on this island the perfect permutations of the change wind blow
right through your head, spinning your eyes like pinwheels and your
mind like a kaleidoscopic nova turns and shatters exposing the starry
fragments of your brain and the light is without the gradations of mercy
and the mind-flowers stir and unfold and your head blooms like
the infinite garden that it really is.
TRESPASSERS BEWARE!   this head is loaded and may go off,
blowing the minds of heedless passers-by, door-to-door messiahs and
daytime somnambulists;

He's the red-handed saint of temptations
He's the ruler of invisible nations
There's a lion walks beside him with a collar made of gold
And the lion whispers secrets that have never been told

He's an angel-eyed gambler who lost all his pride
He's a motorcycle hippie with a thirteen-year-old bride
There's a starburst in his armpit, there's a phoenix in his hand
And he sometimes speaks a language which no one can understand

He's the star-footed dancer of the celestial high-wire
He's the center of a snowstorm with a pocket full of fire
He's the guardian of a lily, he's the father of a flower
He's the hero of a daydream in a crystal-beaded tower

He's the golden-headed vortex of compassionate disaster
He's an arrow of perception and a secret vision master
He's a song-bird in the city, he's a rainbow on the road
He's the trans-substantial messenger, all his movements are in code

He's the jewel-handed brother of illusion
He's yes-and-no at the periphery of fusion
He's the guru of collision, he's the symbol of a rose
He's the instant of sensation and he neither cares nor knows

Holding

there are times the pressure of possessions
becomes almost unbearable
the accumulations of living
bulwarks of rapturous junk
I nestle into velvet
pondering the buoyancy
of begging bowls
The cycle always turns for me
possessions vanish
gradually I learn
things or not-things
it's all alright
it makes no difference
things or not-things
it's all the same

I would not shackle love
bind him to duty
with perfumed schemes and flowered snares
the urgencies of public precedent
or private pain
love grown dutiful is love grown old
a withered cupid faltering at the bow
love, to be love, is free
love is by definition free
and if he choose to go
when I would have him stay
perhaps I'll die a bit
but I'd rather so
than taste his absent minded kiss
and lie uneasy in a masked embrace

If I Am Holy—

if I am holy
    —and I am—
then I am wholly holy

if my left hand is holy
    —and it is—
then my right hand is holy
if my big toe is holy
then my little toe is holy
if my head is holy
then my asshole is holy

if I am holy
    —and I am—
then you are holy
if you are holy
    —and you are—
then all of us are holy

if we are holy
we are the flesh of angels
and the substance of heaven
and the recognition of this is reality
and reality is the infinite domain

I'm writing poems on you
all these kisses   small bites   my hands on you
my tongue tracing starfish on your skin
that's what I'm doing
I've hardly begun
there's a history of springtime I want to lick across your groin
a sparrow song behind your left ear
dawn on a mountain lake across your toes
I am lined with love songs
and I'm scrawling valentines along your cock
It feels so good right now to be a woman, to be a poet
Wait ! I'll tell you about it all the way up your spine

Incarnation of Light

you were Lucifer in the morning
the light bringer, the day star
you were Aurora, tearing Hecate's darkness with your
dancing feet
flaunting your rosegold lushness against the fading night
you were Helios   the sun driver, the flame hero
bright with terrible beauty
you were Hesperus at dusk
first candle of the evening sky

Island

you live *on* an island
surrounded
by sea and sky
a transparent quivering ocean
and the waves crowned in a crash of white
that melts into blue, blue-green, ultramarine and emerald
the sky never stops moving
all day the trade winds blow clouds across each other
shifting the corners of the air
later the darker winds send dreams
crossing the infinite silver of a magician's moon
witch-crazy sister of the vehement sun
that spreads its opulence
over the sea and sands and
the sensate pulsing of flowers
that perfume the morning and the midnight wind
spinning the hearts of the children of men and of angels
into butterfly eternity
where the end of today is tomorrow
and the horizon is bounded by stars

it was your mind that caught me

like to like, the shock of understanding
of no longer a stranger

velvet your mouth that sought me
even as I found you
yes and your eyes that have taught me
of infinite prisms evolving
unfolding the edges of time

Levels

angels of uncommitted time
you do exist
congruent to this wheel of days
at the periphery of circumstance
I've sensed your passage
levels of light
that blow across the rainbow void
remembered visions
of a primal state

love is an art for angels
and we are human, you and I
fallible we are, and fragile
and therefore more than perfect
we take such risks who leap across the void!
perfection is static paradise
but we are human, you and I, and so we dream
and cast our dreams before us
extending our fingertips beyond the finite edge
to brush that certainty
of ringing bliss
that resonates our dreams
impelling us to be that art
which angels strive to emulate

Map of the Moon

It is not the act
        but the concept
not the fulfillment but the vision

not the fire but
        prior knowledge of the flame

answers to which the questions are yet inconceivable

The Mathematics of Love

stopping your mouth with mine
our conversation changes voice
and you and I forget our I and you
lost in that first equation of humanity
that 1 and 1
equals one

Memorabilia

Alice Jo Adams born April 11th of '89 in this house
where morning glories burn against the dry rot wood
now in the intricate parlor
eighty one years
rocks the hours back and forth
rocking away the time in a memory chair
her canary is dead sweetnamed Caruso she fed him on hemp seeds
folding a shawl on his cage
late at night
and lacy hands fondle (mustard gold) a plush covered album
named Schooldays

Be good, Sweet Maid, and let who will be clever
Your Loving Brother,
Thomas J.

When this you see, Remember me
Ada
Lois
Everett
Martha
Millie
Elizabeth Lou

soft dust (the carpet of red rose pale leaves) stirs the air
coating the beaded lamps   the oval photographs
and settling in the open eyes of
the dead old lady
rocking her moonlight hours
in the padlocked house

night passage

the other side of dawn   again
once more I've spanned the oceans of the night
tides of four a.m. despair
and lonely wonders of the dark
beasts of the soul
that lurk behind the silent hours
when wise men sleep at ease
and fools like me
stride mumbling through the stars
dissecting dreams with scalpels of the mind
and bleeding visions
like a wounded ghost
once more I've made it through
pale sunlight warms my skin
small birds that sing in cities light the air
the morning smells so sweet . . . . . .

Nostalgia

nostalgia, like a bathtub of quivering green jello
and me   human fruit salad
great glaucous globs of regurgitated yesterday
adorning me like artificial grapes
just a freewill puppet
strung out on memories
NO WAY I can survive on last year's dinners!
sweet green jello candy rerun is a dangerous drug!!
and this one thing I know for sure—
nothing new ever happens in yesterday

Open Channel

the dream is as true as the dreamer
all fragments of the self are true
and dreams are one more form of sight
are real and not-real
as they move the flesh
and shape the currents of the mind
fears unexorcised and fantasies unsearched
become lame ghosts
visions unreached for
distill a toxin
    aging the spirit
    dimming the flesh
the dream is as true as the dreamer
that which exists within the mind is you
that which contains the mind is you
open your dreams
release your visions and your fantasies and fears
that which is real and not-real
is up to you

the phoenix sings once in five hundred years
distilling silence in a song so pure
music ignites his purple plumaged wings
his straining beak drips fire across the air
and with his final note
he metamorphoses to flame entire
and from that ashy pyre the newborn phoenix soars
to ride the changing winds across the path of time
until his song and he grow ripe again
and the phoenix   little brother of the sun
stretches his heart to the sky

Remembrance of Saint John the Dwarf

saint (fifth century)
of the Egyptian desert
noted
for his simplicity
and absent-mindedness

that which is free
neither gives nor takes   in sacrifice
the sacrifice   an assumption of guilt
an implication of sin   existence as obligation
the ethic of sacrifice, a reflex of fear
a terror of wonder

when we couldn't understand it
either we killed it
or we worshipped it
sometimes
we did both

that which is free remits the code of guilt
and walks in grace

duty : obligation : sin : guilt
fed to the infinite baby
resulted in the finite blame-child
and the expectation of shame
is a blight at the roots of joy

that which is free lives now
committed neither to past nor future
the release of habituation opens the mind
and the hand
and the present becomes   not a bridge
but home

Seven of Stars

I stretch my hand among the stars
and my mind slips through my fingers
forming transient constellations
    shaped like water
    shaped like wind
I am shaped by my vision
and flowers of light ignite from my dream of a hand
a five-fingered star at the end of a wand of bone

Songs of the Blue-Light Dakini

beyond these mountains there are other mountains
    the substance   is of a different texture
stone becomes star   earth becomes cloud
dust becomes prismatic flakes of light

beyond these mountains there are others

beyond this body there are other bodies
    the substance   is of a different texture
flesh becomes space   breath becomes time
senses and perceptions become galaxies

beyond these bodies there are others

sweet love, there are no comparisons
ice is colder, fire is hotter
grass is greener than your eyes
gold is darker than your hair
I can only say about you
knowing you, there are no others
that compare
steel and starlight as your thoughts go
intricate simplicity
gyroscope of balanced madness
graced with wonder, graced with laughter
I can truly say about you
knowing you, there are no others
that compare

Thunder Calliope

THUNDER that cracks the sky
that crashes at your inner ear
demanding paradise forever NOW
THUNDER that breaks the mind
THUNDER that shatters dream, that
hammers at the moving edge of breath

HELL IS AN INVENTION OF THE LIVING

the infinite clock has exploded
the calendar is crumbled on the wind

THUNDER of revelation
THUNDER that sucks the bones of morning

RAINBOW PARADE AND ACROBATS OF TIME

and after thunder
comes lightning

Where It's At: A Melody For Breath

Suppose it's true
Suppose that beyond the cloudpoint of that mountain
there exists a dome contrived of petrified wind
that for a handle on that hidden door
there hangs an eagle's heart
that once a day one drop of blood
falls from that painful flesh
and that the alchemist stands waiting
extending his narrow tongue to lap that bitter blood
and from his single eye there falls one desperate tear
that slides across the sky
a shooting star in someone's magic night

Winter Solstice 1975

The sun stands on the bridge of Capricorn
Saturn's unyielding fulcrum
a tightrope stretched between practical trivia
and the etheric infinity of unleashed spirit,
The Leo moon shakes a proud mane
stirring the king within the chamber of the heart
ambitious, generous & sometimes arrogant.

Brothers and sisters, this time we recognize each other
Extend our hands, expound our visions
Hoping toward harmony
Old angers rise, suppressed resentments surface
Either to cloud the mind
or vanish in a puff of clarity
Kinship is undeniable
Better to deal with each other in respect and love

This is a season of extremes
Sudden gifts and sudden losses
Insights and intuitions both blessing and denying

Idealistic banners will color the winds of winter
The ideals will be tested by storms of reality

There will be change in the concepts of finance
and there will be changes in the change
and the hope will be of harmony
The arts of creation leap in new directions
Unexpected flowers of the mindful heart

Brothers and sisters of blood and of spirit and of circumstance
This is a good time to share our needs & our knowledge
Sharing ourselves with each other is an act of valor and necessity

VI.

A Fictional Sketch

(1953)

The Boy with the Innocent Eyes

The old woman sat quietly on the porch, half dozing as she rocked back and forth. The battered rocking chair gave a small creaking sound as she stirred momentarily and then sank back without awakening. A pattern of shadow-gray and dappled sunlight settled itself upon the network of wrinkles that formed the loose-hanging skin of her face. Her hair was a yellowish-gray mass against the back of the chair, and her puffy, work-worn hands were folded spiritlessly in her lap.

"Who are you?" a shrill, young voice demanded, breaking in on her doze suddenly.

She snapped awake, frightened a little by the sudden noise. She stared at the little figure in front of her, peering intently with her watery, tired eyes. The child was certainly not an alarming figure. He was a small boy, about eight or nine perhaps, and he was possessed of a large quantity of reddish-brown hair and an even larger quantity of freckles. He was wearing brown corduroy pants and a striped tee-shirt, and he had his hands in his pockets.

"Well," he demanded again, more insistently this time, "who are you?"

Her thin bluish lips formed themselves into a smile. "Hello, darling," she said in as warm a tone as was possible in her age-withered vocal cords. "I'm Mrs. Licktman," she continued.

The child stared at her reflectively out of his clear and softly-lashed eyes. "That's an ugly name," he said gently, "and you're an ugly ole woman. I don't think I like you."

The old woman smiled at him hesitantly. "But darling, you don't know what you're saying!" The words came out slowly.

"I do too!" he said instantly, his vanity hurt, "I do too! You're an ugly ole woman and I hate, I hate, I hate you!" He began to jump up and down in front of her, chanting the words in a singsong voice and delighting in the effect they had on her. "Missus Lishman, ugly ole Miss Lishman, ugly ole Missus Lishman!" Suddenly he stood still and looked directly at her for a minute. Then he stuck his tongue out at her and said in a clear simple tone, "I hate you!"

Her lips trembled uncertainly and she pressed her hands closely together. "Darling, you mustn't say things like that, it's not nice. You know you don't mean what you're saying. It's not nice," she repeated.

"I *do* mean what I'm saying," he insisted, and looked at her calmly. "I bet you're the ugliest ole woman in the whole world. And I'm the baddest boy in the whole wide world, and when I grow up I'm going to be a pirate or a gangster or sumpin like that and I'm going to shoot all the ugly ole women there are. And I'm going to shoot you first because you're the ugliest and I hate you." He stood directly in front of her and watched her intently with his innocent blue-gray eyes. She lowered her eyes under his steady stare, and her hand pulled at the folds of her skirt as if for support. Then she smiled at him with false brightness and began to rise.

"Come inside," she offered, "and I'll give you some sugar cookies. I just made them this morning," she added in the same coaxing tone she had used with her own children. He followed her into the cool dark of the parlor and stood there waiting. "Just a minute," she said, "and I'll bring you the cookies." She disappeared into the back of the house and left him standing there.

He looked around the room curiously and then walked over to a glassed-in cabinet filled with souvenirs. He opened one of the doors and pushed his hand in among the carefully dusted gilt figurines and place-named heavy glass ashtrays that filled the shelves. He picked up a shell-encrusted pink one labeled "Atlantic City" but dropped it back on the shelf disinterestedly. He slammed the glass door and sat down on the stiff couch that faced the false fireplace with a mantel filled with old family pictures.

"Here we are!" she announced, hurrying in with a plate of broad sugar-covered cookies and a glass of milk. She sat down next to him on the couch and offered them to him.

He took the glass of milk, and then selected two of the largest and most sugary of the cookies on the plate. "Thank you," he said politely, "but my mother told me never to take more than two." She smiled at him approvingly and put the rest of the cookies on a table in easy reach of the couch, thinking that he was quite a well-mannered boy after all. She relaxed and patted his hand, remembering how she had told her own children the same thing.

He took a large bite out of one of the cookies and then smiled at her confidingly. "You know, you smell bad," he announced. "You smell as if you were half-dead already. And you look like an ole lizard, that's what you look like, an old Lishmun lizard, that's what." She pulled her hand away from him as if she had been holding a burnt-out match that had suddenly burst into flame again. He took another bite of his cookies, washing it down with some milk, while she stared at him disbelievingly.

"How come your hand's so funny looking?" he demanded, comparing his own pink-skinned palm with her shriveled yellow-tipped hand with uneven bluish nails. "And your skin looks like it's going to fall off," he added, taking another bite. "I bet if I pulled hard enough I could pull it all off and then I'd make a drum out of it and beat on it with your ole shin-bone." He finished his cookie and reached for another from the plate, dribbling the crumbs on the spotless rug. "I wish you'd die soon. They'd put you in the ground and the worms would eat you and—"

"Stop, stop!" she screamed. She sank back against the couch weakly. "Darling, you mustn't talk like that, you mustn't, you mustn't," she muttered, looking at him with dazed horror while he took a bite out of a fresh cookie. He stared at her interestedly, startled and pleased with the effect his words had brought about.

She got up from the couch abruptly and walked over to the mantel. She stood there a moment, feeling his sharp young eyes watching her every movement. Then she took down one of the pictures and brought it back to the couch with her. She held it pressed closely to her as she walked, and she looked down at the floor, trying to avoid the boy's unfeelingly curious eyes. She sat down carefully beside him.

"Look," she said softly, holding the picture in its silver frame tenderly in her hands. "This is a picture of my husband and me when we were first married." She held it out to him so that he could see it clearly.

He glanced at the picture boredly, and then knocked it sharply out of her hands. It fell to the floor, the silver frame making a muffled sound as it hit the carpet. A crack appeared in one corner of the glass and then spread until it formed a network of tiny lines over the two faces in the picture. "You were never young," he said positively. Then he made a face at her. "Ole Lishmun-lizard!" he chanted softly, and stuck his tongue out at her. He kicked the picture a little with his foot and then looked at her out of the corner of his eye. He took another bite out of the cookie, waiting for her to say something.

She stared at him dully and then got up, her thin legs trembling so that she had to hold on to the couch for a minute to keep her balance. She stooped over slowly, trying to ease the strain on her back. She picked the picture off the floor and straightened up, looking at the shattered glass wearily. She brushed it off carefully with the sleeve of her dress, and then walked across the room and put it back on the mantel. She didn't look at it again but walked hesitantly back to the couch.

"Why are you so ugly?" he asked. "I never saw anyone as ugly as you before. My mommy's pretty, she's got long brown hair and she puts curls into it. I bet there never was anyone as ugly as you are. You haven't even hardly got any hair and it's all gray and it's just a little bump on your head. I bet if I tried I could pull it off, I'd pull it all out and it'd be all bloody and everything!" He stopped and looked at the old woman. "I think I *will* pull it all out." Her hand went instinctively towards her head and the boy laughed delightedly and stuck his tongue out at her again.

"Come outside," she said, a little of the hope she had had when she asked him to come inside still in her voice, "and I'll show you my flowers. All my life I've been able to raise beautiful flowers," she said a little boastfully. "Every day I water and weed them." She smiled at him, thinking of a poem she had once read and always remembered in which the souls of little children were compared to flowers. His, she thought, must be like some rare flower, difficult to grow, but beautiful when it finally burst into bloom. She looked at his rosy face and smiled at him again, wishing that she could remember the words of the poem, it seemed so true.

"My flowers are the most beautiful things in the world to me," she said as they walked out of the house together. She led him over to the side of the house where there was big bed of carefully tended flowers. "Aren't they lovely?" she said, enthusiasm making her voice come alive again. She looked at them proudly, hoping that he would feel their beauty. "People that pass by, they stop and tell me how wonderful they are to look at, and ask me how I find the time to take such good care of them." He looked at the flowers blankly and then turned to her.

"Are you going to keep on living here?" he demanded.

She nodded silently, hoping that he would say something about her flowers, or go away perhaps.

"I don't like you. Why don't you move somewhere else, or die? If you're going to always live here, then I don't like this house either." Suddenly he moved away from her and bent down. He clasped his hands around a bunch of flowers and began yanking them out, leaving their bare roots showing whitely in the moist soil. He pulled the flowers out hurriedly, throwing them root up on the grass beside him, scattering the dirt indiscriminately.

The old woman stood there stiffly and then began to move towards him, her thin legs with the blue veins trembling a little. "Stop that!" she said, her voice a mixture of pleading and commanding. "Stop that!" The boy looked at her and straightened up. He backed away a little, still clutching a bunch of flowers in his hand. They stood facing each other and he stared at her calmly, but not quite sure what to do next. Then he heard a familiar voice calling him.

"Ronnie!" the voice called insistently, "oh, Ron-nie!"

"That's my mother," he said. He started to move away slowly from the silent figure in front of him. Then he turned and threw the bunch of dirt and flowers toward the motionless old woman, and he ran quickly across the lawn and down the street.

The old woman stared at the torn-up flower bed for a minute and then turned and began slowly and carefully to mount the porch steps, pausing painfully on each one to gather enough strength to reach the next. She stood still for a long moment at the top and then eased herself into the old chair. She began to rock back and forth gently, and as she rocked slow tears began to seep from under her wrinkled eyelids.

Notes

The introduction for this book was written for *Word Alchemy* (New York: Grove Press, 1960) but was not included in the first printing.

The Love Book was first published by Stolen Paper Editions (San Francisco, 1966).

Word Alchemy was first published by Grove Press (New York, 1967). Some of the poems therein had previously appeared in little magazines.

The Three Penny Press writings were originally published in the following chapbooks in the indicated sequence (since the chronology of these publications cannot be determined, the poems appear here in alphabetical order):

> Grover Haynes (ed.), *Beards and Brown Bags* (Studio City, California: Three Penny Press, 1959): "Apogee," "Our morning is afternoon." (Both poems were reprinted in More Beards and Brown Bags in the same year.)
>
> ———, *Beat and Beatific* (Studio City, California: Three Penny Press, 1959): "Hey, hey, I have a universe to share with you," "My beloved has a hundred faces . . . ," "The Twenty Nine Hungers of God."

Lenore Kandel, *An Exquisite Navel* (Studio City, California: Three Penny Press, 1959): "All I have in the world," "Clearly beloved, we are huddled here together," "Home is where you find it," "I thought you were a man," "Mountains and cities and pitfalls and," "Slipping into my heart as once," "There is a hole in my heart," "This is my world," "Your conversation, friend."

———, *A Passing Dragon* (two editions: n.p.: Three Penny Press, 1959, and Studio City, California: Three Penny Press, 1959): "A Passing Dragon," "Hungry as a sulky child nothing suits me," "I gave you all the rains," "I have chosen for my guide the gray wind," "I have fallen in love with the wind," "Loving and love being the reason behind it all," "My love gave me an orange tree," "Oh, my beloved," "Such a tomcat then," "The hot wind blows and I wish I could blow with it," "You are like a lion," "You there! You with the loneliness."

———, *Poetry: Restricted: An Exquisite Navel* (Studio City, California: Three Penny Press, 1959): "Pigeons always spell New York to me," "The love I had for you, baby."

The poems in the section called "Poems from Little Magazines and Broadsides" originally appeared as follows:

"A Place to Stand" a Sore Dove Press broadside (2004) and *The Café Review* 16 (Winter 2005)

"afraid to sleep alone" *El Corno Emplumado/The Plumed Horn* 11 (July 1964)

"Afternoon of a Phoenix" *The Fiddlehead* 58 (Fall 1963)

"Ah love, I had not meant to leave" *The Galley Sail Review* 11, vol. 4, no. 1 (November 1962)

"Baby listen, I am the missionary of love" *Beatitude* 17 (October–November 1960)

"Changeling" *The Fiddlehead* 51 (Winter 1962)

"City Night" *Bitterroot* 1, no. 1 (Fall 1962)

"Dead Billy" *Io* 23 (1976)

"dry man" *Io* 23 (1976)

"Epilogue" *The Fiddlehead* 61 (Summer 1964)

"Everyday Magic" *City Miner* 12, vol. 4, no. 1 (1979)

"Excerpt from a Prayer Wheel" *Notes from Underground* 3 (ca. 1969)

"Fog-Bound" *Bitterroot* 2, no. 5 (Fall 1963)

"Fuck/Angel" *Femora* 2 (1964)

"girl story" *The Fiddlehead* 58 (Fall 1963)

"Grant Avenue" *EPOS* 15, no. 3 (Spring 1964)

"Gregory . . . ." *Poetry Flash* no. 287 (April/May 2001)

"Grey-Beast" *The Fiddlehead* 51 (Winter 1962)

"Hawaiian Mountain" *Mele* 11 (March 1969)

"Hero the Rider" *FUCK YOU/a magazine of the arts* no. 5, vol. 3 (May 1963)

"Hymn to Maitreya in America" *The Floating Bear: a newsletter* no. 37 (March–July 1969)

"I have never seen a nightingale" *Coastlines* 18, vol. 5, no. 2 (1962)

“I reveal my belly to delight” *Theo* 1, no. 1 (ca. 1964)

“If all day long you had a perfectly beautiful Tuesday” *Yowl* 5 (1964)

“In the Bitter Hours of Night” *EPOS* 14, no. 3 (Spring 1963)

“Muir Beach Mythology/September” *The Outsider* 4/5 (1969)

“Museum Concert” Poems Accepted for *Genesis West:* A Supplement (August 1964)

“my love the fisherman comes back smelling of salt dying” Poems Accepted for *Genesis West:* A Supplement (August 1964)

“No Clock No Time” *Blue Beat* 1 (March 1964)

“Old Lady Poem” *EPOS* 15, no. 2 (Winter 1963–64)

“Old men practice misdirection on the young men” *Open City* 52 (Renaissance Supplement) (May 1–14, 1968)

“Phoenix Song” *The Fiddlehead* 58 (Fall 1963)

“Poem for a Long-Gone Lover” *The Fiddlehead* 60 (Spring 1964)

“Poem for Ann” *EPOS* 12, no. 4 (Summer 1961)

“Poem for Sunday Riders” *The Fiddlehead* 62 (Fall 1964)

“prayer on the wind” *Io* 23 (1976)

“Quantum Choreography” *City Miner* 12, vol. 4 no. 1 (1979)

“Rebirth” *Lynx* 1, no. 1 (January 1962)

"Rocking in the rain" *San Francisco Review* 1, no. 10 (December 1961)

"Rose Dream" *EPOS* 16, no. 4 (Summer 1965)

"Scarey Song" *The Fiddlehead* 51 (Winter 1962)

"seven of velvet" *Io* 23 (1976)

"Small Hours Poem" *El Corno Emplumado/The Plumed Horn* 11 (July 1964)

"Someday When We Are Strangers" *Coastlines* 18, vol. 5, no. 2 (1962)

"Speaking of . . ." *Beatitude* 16 (July 13, 1960)

"Storm July" *The Fiddlehead* 61 (Summer 1964)

"Steazoned in heazell, by candlelight" *San Francisco Review* 1, no. 10 (December 1961)

"sweet love I have lost my words lost my praises" *The Fiddlehead* 61 (Summer 1964)

"the pot bird story" *Shaman Woman, Mainline Lady: Women's Writings on the Drug Experience*, ed. Cynthia Palmer and Michael Horowitz (New York: Quill, 1982)

"The Time of the Golden Bull" *The Fiddlehead* 57 (Summer 1963)

"Vernal Equinox Forecast—1968" *A Free City News Broadside* (1968)

"Watching the Veiled Moon" *The Fiddlehead* 51 (Winter 1962)

"Witch Song" *The Fiddlehead* 51 (Winter 1962)

“Wonder Wander” *EPOS* 12, no. 4 (Summer 1961)

“Woods Poem” *The Fiddlehead* 51 (Winter 1962)

The unpublished works appear courtesy of the author’s estate.

“The Boy with the Innocent Eyes” was first published in *American Vanguard* 1953, ed. Charles I. Glicksberg and Brom Weber (New York: Dial Press).

Alphabetical List of Works

A Definition of Love 194
A Passing Dragon 97
A Place to Stand 181
"afraid to sleep alone" 149
Afternoon of a Phoenix 138
Afterword 185
Age of Consent 24
"Ah love, I had not meant to leave" 130
"All I have in the world" 77
American Dreams 186
Anatomy Note 43
Angel 190
Apogee 79

"Baby listen, I am the missionary of love" 115
Beast Parade 12
Bedsong for Her 45
Blues for Sister Sally 56
Bus Ride 42

Changeling 121
Cherokee 191

CircumLocation 192
Circus 11
City Night 129
"Clearly beloved, we are huddled here together" 80

Dancers Poem 193
Dead Billy 173
Dope Poem 195
dry man 174

Emerald Poem 27
Enlightenment Poem 18
Epilogue 153
Eros/Poem 33
Everyday Magic 178
Excerpt 196
Excerpt from a Prayer Wheel 171

Farewell to Fancy 21
First They Slaughtered the Angels 28
Fog-Bound 141
Freak Show and Finale 16
Fuck/Angel 156

girl story 140
God/Love Poem 3
Grant Avenue 147
Gregory 180
Grey-Beast 125

Hard Core Love 34
Hawaiian Mountain 165
"He's the red-handed saint of temptations" 197
Hero the Rider 132

"Hey, hey, I have a universe to share with you" 81
Holding 198
"Home is where you find it" 82
Horoscope 70
"Hungry as a sulky child nothing suits me" 84
Hymn to Maitreya in America 167

"I gave you all the rains" 85
"I have chosen for my guide the gray wind" 86
"I have fallen in love with the wind" 87
"I have never seen a nightingale" 128
"I reveal my belly to delight" 148
"I thought you were a man" 88
"I would not shackle love" 199
"If all day long you had a perfectly beautiful Tuesday" 158
If I Am Holy— 200
"I'm writing poems on you" 201
In the Bitter Hours of Night 131
In the Comics 67
In Transit 64
Incarnation of Light 202
Invocation and Clowns, Dance of the Bareback Riders 15
Invocation for Maitreya 17
Island 203
"it was your mind that caught me" 204

Joy Song 32
Junk/Angel 55

Kirby/Poem 54

Lady/Poem 25
Levels 205

Love in the Middle of the Air 14
"love is an art for angels" 206
Love-Lust Poem 35
Love Song for Snow White 44
"Loving and love being the reason behind it all" 90

Map of the Moon 207
Melody for Married Men 48
Memorabilia 209
Morning Song 58
"Mountains and cities and pitfalls and" 91
Muir Beach Mythology/September 170
Museum Concert 155
"My beloved has a hundred faces . . ." 92
"My love gave me an orange tree" 93
"my love the fisherman comes back smelling of salt dying" 154

Naked I Have Known You 52
night passage 210
No Clock No Time 143
Nostalgia 211
Now Vision 19

"Oh, my beloved" 94
Old Lady Poem 142
"old men" 161
Open Channel 212
"Our morning is afternoon" 95

Peyote Walk 37
Phoenix Song 139
"Pigeons always spell New York to me" 98
Poem for a Long-Gone Lover 146

Poem for Ann 117
Poem for Perverts 72
Poem for Peter 46
Poem for Sunday Riders 157
Poem for Tyrants 40
Poster 11
prayer on the wind 175

Quantum Choreography 177

Rebirth 120
Remembrance of Saint John the Dwarf 214
"Rocking in the rain" 118
Rose/Vision 23
Rose Dream 159

Scarey Song 122
Seven of Stars 215
seven of velvet 176
"Slipping into my heart as once" 99
Small Hours Poem 150
Small Prayer for Falling Angels 51
Someday When We Are Strangers 127
Songs of the Blue-Light Dakini 216
Speaking of . . . 113
Spring 61 49
"Steazoned in heazell, by candlelight" 119
Stonedream 26
Storm July 151
"Such a tomcat then" 102
"sweet love, there are no comparisons" 217
"sweet love I have lost my words lost my praises" 152

Telephone from a Madhouse 60
The Boy with the Innocent Eyes 223
The Farmer, the Sailor 41
"The hot wind blows and I wish I could blow with it" 83
"The love I had for you, baby" 89
The Mathematics of Love 208
"the phoenix sings once in five hundred years" 213
the pot bird story 179
The Time of the Golden Bull 133
The Twenty Nine Hungers of God 106
"There is a hole in my heart" 103
"This is my world" 104
Three/Love Poem 47
Thunder Calliope 218
To Fuck with Love Phase I 5
To Fuck with Love Phase II 6
To Fuck with Love Phase III 7

Vernal Equinox Forecast—1968 160
Vision of the Skull of the Prophet 39

Watching the Veiled Moon 123
Were–Poem 22
Where It's At: A Melody For Breath 219
Winter Solstice 1975 220
Witch Song 124
Wonder Wander 116
Woods Poem 126

"You are like a lion" 107
"Your conversation, friend" 109
"You there! You with the loneliness" 108

About the Author

Lenore Kandel was born in New York City in 1932. Her father, novelist and screenwriter Aben Kandel, moved his family to Los Angeles soon after Lenore was born. By twelve, Lenore was reading about Buddhism and world religion, and beginning to write. As a young woman, she took courses at the New School for Social Research in New York. Her first published works were issued in 1959 by Three Penny Press in North Hollywood.

She returned to California in 1960, this time settling in San Francisco, where she initially lived in the co-op East-West House, home to many key poets and a spontaneous meeting place for readings and conversation with writers, filmmakers, and visual artists. Lew Welch lived there, as did Cid Corman. Lawrence Ferlinghetti, Jack Kerouac, Peter Coyote, and filmmakers Jack Smith and Kenneth Anger visited.

In November 1964, Kandel read at the University of California Poetry Conference, organized by Charles Olson. On her thirty-fifth birthday, just before the Summer of Love, she read at the 1967 Great Human Be-In in Golden Gate Park, sharing the stage with Allen Ginsberg, Timothy Leary, and Michael McClure, who later told the *San Francisco Chronicle,* "The entire crowd of 20,000 or 30,000 people sang 'Happy Birthday' to her."

Kandel came to national attention in late 1966, when copies of her poetic suite *The Love Book* were confiscated on the grounds of obscenity during a police raid of San Francisco's City Lights bookstore and the Psychedelic Shop. The protracted trial persisted until the work was finally cleared by a federal court in 1974.

Lenore Kandel was a lifelong member of the political activist group the Diggers, organizing and sourcing free food, medical care, and shelter, and organizing Digger poetry readings. She had a cameo role in Kenneth Anger's 1967 film *Lucifer Rising* and played The Deaconess in his *Invocation of My Demon Brother* (1969).

In 1970, she and her boyfriend, Hell's Angel Bill "Sweet William" Fritsch, were involved in a serious motorcycle crash that left her permanently disabled. A German translation of her two books, *Das Liebesbuch/Wortalchemie,* appeared in 2005. She continued to write until her death on October 18, 2009.

The Io Poetry Series

The Io Poetry Series honors the career work of poets who express the depth, breadth, and scope of subject matter of *Io* and North Atlantic Books. The Series pays tribute to North Atlantic Books' literary roots in *Io*, the interdisciplinary journal founded by Lindy Hough, Richard Grossinger, and colleagues in 1964. *Io*'s single-subject issues laid the groundwork for North Atlantic Books' literary publishing of subsequent decades. The poets in this series either appeared in the journal, were working concurrently, or preceded and inspired *Io*.

Westport Poems
JONATHAN TOWERS

Heavenly Tree, Northern Earth
GERRIT LANSING

The Intent On: Collected Poems, 1962–2006
KENNETH IRBY

Wild Horses, Wild Dreams: New and Selected Poems, 1971–2010
LINDY HOUGH

Collected Poems of Lenore Kandel
LENORE KANDEL